MW00464750

# Broken Spirit

# to

# Boundless Joy

## How to Break Through Your Hurts And Take Back Your Life

*Based on a True Story*

## Kathy Bates

Copyright ©2019 Psalm 23 Ministries

All rights reserved. No part of this publication may be reproduced, distributed, or transmitted in any form or by any means, including photocopying, recording, or other electronic or mechanical methods, without the prior written permission of the publisher, except in the case of brief quotations embodied in reviews and certain other non-commercial uses permitted by copyright law.

All scripture quoted in this book are indicated by the translation it came from (listed below), using Bible Gateway online Bible version as the source at Biblegateway.com

**New International Version (NIV)**
Holy Bible, New International Version®, NIV® Copyright ©1973, 1978, 1984, 2011 by Biblica, Inc.® Used by permission. All rights reserved worldwide.

**Living Bible (TLB)**
The Living Bible Copyright © 1971 by Tyndale House Foundation. Used by permission of Tyndale House Publishers Inc., Carol Stream, Illinois 60188. All rights reserved.

**New King James Version (NKJV)**
Scripture taken from the New King James Version®. Copyright © 1982 by Thomas Nelson. Used by permission. All rights reserved.

**English Standard Version (ESV)**
The Holy Bible, English Standard Version. ESV® Text Edition: 2016. Copyright © 2001 by Crossway Bibles, a publishing ministry of Good News Publishers.

**New American Standard Bible (NASB)**
Copyright © 1960, 1962, 1963, 1968, 1971, 1972, 1973, 1975, 1977, 1995 by The Lockman Foundation

The publisher is not responsible for websites (or their content) that are not owned by the publisher.

ISBN: 978-1-7337237-0-1

# Dedication

*I would like to dedicate this book to every person who has suffered abuse and sexual assault. Please know that you do not have to suffer in silence, there are many resources to help you. There is hope of a normal life again filled with peace and joy! Jesus Christ is your redeemer and through Him restoration is possible.*

# Acknowledgements

**I would like to thank the following for their support:**

Duane—My amazing husband who had more faith in me than I did. Thank you for letting me bounce ideas off of you and all the help and support you gave me along the way. I am blessed to call you my husband!

Pastor Greg—For being my spiritual advisor on this book and being a friend for decades! I hold high regard for your counsel and value our friendship.

Mary and Scott—For sharing your story of heartache turned into triumph through Jesus Christ and in turn helping others restore their lives.

Brian—Thank you for being vulnerable and sharing your difficult story. I believe it will instill hope in others who have suffered this type of trauma.

Julie—Thank you for sharing a story that is still raw and ongoing. I know it will help others in similar situations.

# Contents

# Foreword

Kathy not only survived, but she has thrived! I knew Kathy several years prior to the events of this story, as she had been a member of the church I pastored. Upon moving to another pastorate a few states away, I was outside looking in, at a once-vibrant life that began to crumble under extreme circumstances.

This is a story of tragic events. In these pages, you will encounter an emotional roller coaster of abuse, betrayal, pain, confusion and rejection. You will also encounter hope, peace, spiritual resolve, blessing and ultimate victory. All exist in this story. Above all, you will come face to face with spiritual grit, born out of a tenacious grip of her trust in Jesus Christ. The enemy of our souls does not like stories that end this way. I rejoice that it did.

Scripture reads in **Genesis 50:20 (NIV):** *You intended to harm me, but God intended it for good to accomplish what is now being done, the saving of many lives.*

Kathy realizes she is not the only person who is or has experienced what she went through. I know Kathy's greatest hope is that as you read her story, if you find yourself living out the same torment or perhaps you have landed somewhere on the other side but still unsettled, she desires that you will find strength to face another day. She did. You can too.

**Joel 2:25 (NKJV):** *So I will restore to you the years...*

How God can take what Satan meant and intended for evil and turn it into something beautiful and good is the miracle evidenced in this story. So, sit back, buckle up. In the following pages you will encounter turbulence, but through God's grace, you'll also witness a smooth landing.

Greg Eilders, Senior Pastor
Peoples Church
Bourbonnais, IL

February 24, 2019

# Introduction

Have you ever been hurt by another person? If you are honest with yourself, the answer is yes. We have all been hurt at one point, some of those hurts are greater than others. Dealing with emotions caused by a deep hurt can be a difficult task. The wounds can go so deep that one doesn't know how to process what they are feeling. In this book I will help you identify those emotions, why you feel that way, and give you steps to help you start your healing process.

Throughout the book I share with you my personal stories of betrayal, abuse and the deep hurts I experienced because of these things. I share with you how these life-changing events shattered my life and my hope. You will experience the journey I took to healing and rebuilding my life. This includes the road I traveled to reach forgiveness, and eventually be able to leave the past behind me. And you will learn of God's grace, love and His desire to be with you always.

If you want to feel "normal" and wish you could get rid of the gut-wrenching hurt that you are experiencing, this book will be a guide to start that process. You will learn that healing takes time, and there is a right way and a wrong way to handle your emotions.

I feel confident that if you follow the steps outlined, and allow the Lord to work in you, that you will feel release and begin to hope again. However, I want to prepare you upfront that the process is not easy, but the investment is well worth the reward. It may not seem like you could ever be happy again or live a life with peace and contentment. That is a normal reaction to trauma, but I am here to give you hope, as a survivor of trauma myself.

The process of healing from your pain will require patience with yourself, God and others. You will need to learn to trust the process and put deep trust in the Lord. We all want the pain to go away instantly, but that won't happen, so be prepared for that. The good news is you are not alone, and God will minister to you throughout your journey, if you let Him.

I am so thankful for Jesus being in my life. I hate to think where my life would be without His grace, mercy and amazing love for me. Sharing what I went through and what the Lord taught me is humbling. It blesses me to know that my suffering could be turned into a blessing to help others heal from their suffering.

The names mentioned in this book (other than ministries, references and those with permission) have been changed to protect the privacy of these people and their families. It is not my intention to name names, or to expose who did what. That would defeat the purpose of this book.

Are you ready to start this journey? If you are seeking a change in your life, then I ask that you keep an open mind and heart to the principles I share. They are all biblically based, and can transform you if they are applied. Let's get started in helping you take back your life

# Chapter 1
# A Birthday Not to Remember

It was only a few days away from my birthday and normally I would have been so excited. I'm one of these people that loves to celebrate my birthday. But this year, things were a little strained. Aside from that, this first weekend of October 1994 started off somewhat typical, as in other years. My husband, Brett, always spent this weekend away at his parent's home, for the opening season of duck hunting. He and his dad loved to go hunting together. This year was no different and I usually went with him to spend time with his mom. Often, we would go antique shopping and just have girl time. After the guys returned from hunting, the four of us would celebrate my birthday, and my in-law's wedding anniversary, which happened to be the same day as my birthday.

But this year I decided not to go with Brett because we were having some marital issues, and

I thought the time away from each other might be good. He was to return home Sunday evening, Oct 2nd. The time to myself was reflective and peaceful. It was nice not having the stress of fighting for a couple of days. On Sunday morning I got up and went to church, just as I normally did. When I returned home, I was met with an unexpected find.

Upon walking into my home, I stood there stunned with my mouth hanging open, I thought I had been robbed. Looking around I noticed furniture was missing. As I proceeded to walk through the house, room by room, I took a mental inventory. The spare bed was gone. I looked in the closet and all of his clothes were gone.

Brett moved out and took what he wanted with him, all while I was at church. He knew I was faithful to attend church each Sunday, so he lined up some friends and a moving truck for that morning. They patiently waited around the corner, out of view, until they saw me drive off. Then they worked quickly to load up the truck and get out of there before I returned.

Once I got over the initial shock and realized I hadn't been robbed, but that my husband took these things, I was so angry. How could he be so cowardly as to do this while I was at church? Nothing like taking advantage of someone's faith! It's not like I didn't know we had problems in our marriage. It just would have been nice if he could have told me face to face that he was planning to move out. This is called running from your problems rather than facing them head on.

Backtrack to about June of 1994, a day that is very vivid in my mind, all these years later. We were in the car together, and we just could not get along. When we got home, I asked him what was wrong with him; then out of nowhere I blurted out, "Are you having an affair?" I don't know what made me say that! The silent pause came next, which made me fear his answer. The silence was broken by that dreaded word, yes. My world crumbled around me in that instant.

As faithful as God is, He was trying to prepare me for this moment. A few weeks prior to Brett admitting the affair, I had a dream about him. In that dream I saw Brett with another woman with long, dark hair in the car together. When I told him about the dream, the look on his face was as if he saw a ghost. His response was, "Why would you dream something like that?" Of course, I asked him if it were true and he denied it. At the time I didn't suspect him of having an affair, so I believed him. Who hasn't had a weird dream that made no sense? It wasn't until that yes answer that I realized that the dream I had was from God.

After finding out Brett had cheated on me, the next few days were a blur of emotions. I felt so betrayed. Brett and I talked a few days later and he said he wanted to work things out. I am a firm believer of honoring marriage vows, which means there may be some better and worse moments. As hard as it was to make myself any more vulnerable, I agreed to give him another chance. We knew we needed some help, so we decided to meet with our pastor. He pointed out to Brett that he needed to be accountable to me. His betrayal had broken my trust and now he would have to work at getting it back. That meant he would have to be willing to let me know where he was at all times (if that was what I needed). Things went well for a while, even though he struggled with the accountability aspect.

In the meantime, this woman kept calling Brett and trying to see him. So, he felt we needed to getaway for a weekend. Brett's parents were going to be out of town, so we decided to "hide out" at their place. Brett asked me to keep checking his voicemail throughout the weekend in case she would leave him a message. Apparently, she had been calling several times a day and leaving him messages, because he was not answering her calls. Brett did not want to hear her voice and asked me to delete any messages from her. Thinking back, that's a hard thing to ask your wife to do, but at the same time, he knew he was weak and needed that help. I was just happy that he was making an effort to save our marriage.

Unfortunately, the rebuilding attempt did not last long, maybe 4 months at the most. At some point the constant pursuing from that seducing spirit wore him down. Don't get me wrong, I am not defending Brett. He was a grown man, capable of making his own decisions. I'm just saying he gave in to the temptation. It takes two to tango, which in this case both were guilty of their wrong decisions. The devil works hard through temptation to bring people down. Seducing spirits are very real and very dangerous. Therefore, it is always important to guard your heart and mind to avoid falling prey to sexual immorality.

Scripture warns of temptation as well as a seductress. Listed below are a few scriptures to support this:

**Matthew 26:41(NKJV) and Mark 14:38 (NKJV):** *Watch and pray, lest you enter into temptation. The spirit indeed is willing, but the flesh is weak.*

**Luke 8:13 (NKJV):** *But the ones on the rock are those who, when they hear, receive the word with joy; and these have no root, who believe for a while and in time of temptation fall away.*

**1 Corinthians 10:13 (NKJV):** *No temptation has overtaken you except such as is common to man; but God is faithful, who will not allow you to be tempted beyond what you are able, but with the temptation will also make the way of escape, that you may be able to bear it.*

**Proverbs 2:16 (NKJV):** *To deliver you from the immoral woman, from the seductress who flatters with her word.*

**Proverbs 4:23 (NKJV):** *Above all else, guard your heart, for everything you do flows from it.*

Additional scriptures to look up include: Luke 22:46, James 1:12, Proverbs 6:24 and Proverbs 23:27.

Not being able to resist that temptation any longer was the final "nail in the coffin" of our marriage. After discovering Brett had moved out and this was my new reality, the emotions started flooding in. What am I going to do now? How will I make it on my own? I felt betrayal, anger, and even felt hatred for this other woman.

I recall crying out with tears to God, "Why can't he love me? Why? Why am I so unlovable?" I was filled with questions and felt scared and alone. At one point I was sobbing so hard that I was gasping for breath. This pain was something I had never experienced before.

## What Else Could Go Wrong?

As my world was spiraling out of control that Sunday and Monday, unfortunately it was only the beginning to yet another trauma. Brett and I had agreed to meet on the evening of Tuesday,

October 4th. It was a very uncomfortable meeting, as we talked about his decision. We went our separate ways, with him wanting a divorce. It was almost midnight when I arrived home to an empty house. Crying and distraught, I got ready for bed. Suddenly, I heard a noise at the door. I thought Brett had come in the house, but I couldn't understand why he would let himself in, considering the situation. With tears streaming down my face, I went to see what he wanted. Standing at the top of the stairs looking down at the front door, I saw him slipping on the throw rug, with hands outstretched to catch himself from falling. When he looked up at me, I suddenly realized it wasn't Brett!

Frozen in fear, I just stood there. After what seemed like minutes, but was only seconds, I screamed, "Who are you?" That doesn't seem like the first words one would say, but it was my first response. I can still see that image in my head and recall it vividly!

Upon regaining his balance, he came running up the stairs. As he pushed me up against the wall, with his hand over my mouth, he told me to shut up. Then he pushed me into the bedroom and assaulted me. My world stopped. I was terrified! It is hard to even put into words how I felt. As he was leaving, he told me not to call anyone until he left the house. Being so afraid and in shock, I waited a short time, then called 9-1-1.

The police arrived and canvased the neighborhood but could not find him. They collected evidence and took my statement. I had recognized the guy as someone we had hired to do some painting in the house, the nephew of a friend of Brett. But I couldn't remember his name. Looking back, I believe this is the reason I had asked him who he was. My brain recognized him but couldn't recall his name.

As the police were questioning me, I realized that Brett would have all the information the police would need, so I gave them his phone number. The police called Brett from my kitchen, as I sat at the snack bar listening in. I could hear his mistress in the background having a fit. After the officer hung up the phone, he made some comment to the effect of, "She's a piece of work." I guess she was accusing me of lying, making this whole thing up to get Brett back. What did Brett see in this woman?

As it turns out, this guy was also one of the guys who helped Brett move out of the house just two days earlier. He knew I would be alone and he knew how to access my home. We had a dog kennel in the garage with a doggie door accessing the kennel outside. He also knew that Brett had taken the dog with him. So, he crawled through the doggie door from the outside kennel into the garage, then accessed the house from the garage entrance. This was not a door we ever locked, and I believe many people don't. Please lock your doors, especially if there is another way someone could access your garage!

While at the house, the police asked if there was anyone they could call for me. They suggested I have someone come over or I go stay with them. I gave them my friend, Teri's name and number, so they called her. She came over and picked me up and took me to stay at her house. That was a sleepless night, as I laid in bed and wept.

The next morning Brett called to check up on me. I told him I was staying at Teri's house for a day or two. He showed up at her house wanting to see me. She was *not* going to let him in, what a great body guard! But Brett was persistent. So, Teri made him wait outside while she came and talked to me to let me know he was there. All I had to do was say the word and she would make him go away. But I wanted him to face me, so I said let him in. I told him what I thought of his girlfriend, accusing me of faking this whole thing. He agreed and apologized. One could only hope this would have been a wake-up call for Brett, but it wasn't.

From the time of this writing, this whole incident happened almost exactly 24 years ago. Yet, some of the images in my head are still very vivid as if they happened recently. And the reason I remember the dates so well is because October 5th is my birthday, and this is what I got for my birthday in 1994! Thankfully, I have never let this trauma affect my birthday.

Fear crept in and took over my life. I slept with all the lights on, every door and window locked. One evening I heard a noise that sounded like someone turning the basement doorknob. My heart was racing. I called 9-1-1 again, as they told me to do the night of the attack. They came and checked the house inside and out and found nothing. I apologized for calling them, feeling like I had overreacted. But they were so understanding and said that is what they were there for, and to call anytime that I felt unsafe. They even offered to do extra patrol in my neighborhood.

I did not know how to regain a sense of safety. Before this had happened, I had never experienced anything so terrifying. The paranoia did not go away quickly, even after moving back to North Dakota, my home state. Many times, I found myself tensing up as I walked to my car after work if there was a guy anywhere near me. Any time I saw a guy that resembled the man who attacked me, fear washed over me. It took a very long time before I started to relax.

## Justice?

This is one of those life-altering events I mentioned in the Introduction. It changed the way I trusted men, questioning their motives. It changed the way I lived, locking doors and windows and sleeping with lights on. I grew up in a small town where life was good and people were nice. I never thought this would happen to me—but it did. Life would never be the same as I knew it, and I needed to find a new normal.

So here I was, living hundreds of miles away from my family, faced with a divorce and now a court case for assault. I was the victim of an attempted rape, and I did not know how to cope.

Two things I never thought would happen to me, happened all at the same time.

In case you were wondering, yes, the attacker was convicted. He was given the maximum sentence for attempted rape, which was only 3.5 years. That does not seem right for an act that forever altered my life, but that was the law. On the night of the attack I had shared with the police something that would end up being a key piece of evidence. I had told them I had cleaned my house earlier that day. However, after the attacker left, there was straw from the dog kennel scattered about the foyer. When the police went to talk to him, they noticed the coat he wore the night of the attack had straw in the pockets. I can't say for sure if that was the *gottcha* moment, but he made a full confession. Thankfully, I did not have to go to court. What a relief that was!

I was given the opportunity to write a Victim's Impact Statement to mail to the District Attorney that would be read in court. Though I lived scared for a long time, somehow God gave me the strength to forgive this man. I'm not even sure what process I went through to make that decision. I told him in the statement that I forgave him, but my forgiveness did not excuse him for what he did. I prayed that he would give his life to Jesus. Honestly, I don't think I have ever held a grudge against him, which I attribute to being able to forgive him. Forgiveness is freeing, and I will discuss this more in Chapter 8 and 9.

How could I forgive this man that hurt me, violated me, instilled fear into me? I wish I could say forgiveness has always come this easy for me, but it hasn't. Learning to forgive Brett and his mistress certainly did not come easy. That took years! But my biggest test in learning forgiveness came years later through yet another trauma in my life, which I will discuss in later chapters, along with the process I had to go through to finally reach forgiveness.

# Chapter 2
# Gamut of Emotions

Even though I forgave this man rather quickly, much to my own surprise, it doesn't mean I didn't go through a whole gamut of emotions. We all experience a variety of emotions, triggered by something good or bad. They are as natural as the breath you take. How you handle your emotions is what I want to address. I am going to break down some of the things I felt after this very difficult time in my life. As you read through them, ask yourself if this is something you have struggled with.

## Shock

The first emotion I felt was shock after finding out my husband was having an affair. I also felt shock when I came home to find he had moved out. Then again, even more shock after seeing a strange man in my house, and finally the shock of being assaulted. In all four incidents, I didn't want to believe what was happening. My mind could not wrap itself around these events. I kept hoping I would wake up from this bad dream. Instead, it was like an earthquake, with each aftershock causing more pain.

You may have experienced shock when something unexpected or overwhelming took place. Shock can be both good and bad. For instance, you may be shocked to learn that you won the lottery, or you got a job promotion that you weren't expecting. Those are exciting, good shocks to have! On the other hand, a shock triggered by a hurtful experience can be followed by many unhealthy feelings.

Whether you are male or female, you are not exempt from feeling shock, or any other emotion for that matter. However, it seems that men sometimes don't show their emotions as much as women, but it doesn't mean you don't feel them. Shock is a natural feeling as well as a physical response to trauma. The severity of the shock all depends on what you go through. Suppressing your feelings will only compound the hurt. Crying and allowing yourself to express how you feel is very therapeutic.

It is important to mention that your loved ones may also experience shock, even if they are not the direct victim of a trauma. An event like this also affects them in some way. So, they may need healing right alongside you. They may also need your patience and understanding as much as you need that from them. No matter what your story is, the process of dealing with emotions is often the same.

## Fear

Fear is a very complex emotion that encompasses many levels of response. Do you recall ever saying things like "What if I can't?" or "How will I be able to...." or "Where will I go from here?" Also, you may have questioned yourself thinking, "I don't think I can do this," or "I'm scared," or even "I'm not strong enough or good enough." These are all doubtful phrases that are rooted in fear.

Fear can become very paralyzing when you let it consume your thoughts. Even when your life is going great, you never have complete control over your life. You don't know what is going to happen from moment to moment. But when something happens to disrupt your normal way of life, you suddenly think you've lost control, when you never really had it in the first place. Panic or fear can then set in causing you to react negatively.

One night, Teri invited me and several close friends over to her house for a small party. We played games, had a good time and enjoyed lots of laughs. These were good friends trying to cheer me up. Still apprehensive, one of my friends, Brad, offered to follow me home and check out the house for me. When we arrived, I saw that I had a message on the answering machine. What came next was *not* what I was expecting. It was the voice of my attacker. I don't recall what he said, but I immediately began to tremble and cry. Brad gave me a hug and tried to comfort me. He offered to stay the night to help me feel safe; I should have accepted his offer but didn't. No, this was not a boyfriend, just a friend stepping up to the plate, trying to protect me. I think I just wanted to bawl all night and didn't want to expose him to that. Sleep was nonexistent for me again that night.

The next day I reported this incident to the police, and they asked me to drop off the tape from the recorder to the detective. This was only a few days after the initial attack and the police still hadn't talked to the attacker yet. Even with all his contact information, they wanted to wait for the right time, whenever that was. They said they wanted to get a confession out of him. I'm guessing they were waiting to get all their "ducks in a row" with as much evidence as possible. I don't recall how long that was, a week or two maybe, but it seemed like eternity.

I was frustrated with them at the time because it made no sense to me. Why don't they arrest him? I didn't feel safe with him roaming around. As I mentioned I slept with the lights on...in every room! I even thought about sleeping with a hammer by my bed, but then I realized if he comes back, he is stronger than me and might use it on me. As I mentioned in Chapter 1, the police did get him to confess. Sometimes we just need to trust the process.

Have you ever felt so scared you didn't know what to do? The man who attacked me had not been arrested yet and I was desperate to feel some sense of security. I needed our dog back, hoping she would give that sense of safety. Brandi was a beautiful yellow lab that Brett had bought to take hunting with him. I never was much of a dog lover, but we had Brandi since she was a puppy, so I grew somewhat attached. Since

Brett had taken her when he moved out, I had to convince him to let me have her back for a while. He agreed, but he had a hunting trip planned so he wanted to keep her until after that trip. I was so scared one night that I couldn't wait, so I drove over to where he was living and took Brandi out of the kennel and drove around town looking for a hotel. But most hotels at that time would not accept a dog, so I finally mustered up enough courage to return home.

Brandi did help me to feel safer and a bit calmer. I recall one evening I was watching a TV show when someone on the show started to cry. The house I lived in was a multi-level home. I was sitting up in the living room, which overlooked the front door area, where Brandi was laying on the rug, the same rug the attacker slipped on. When the crying started, she looked up at me with those big brown eyes, asking me if I was OK. Amazingly enough when I said I was OK, and that it wasn't me, she seemed to understand and laid her head back down. She had heard me cry so much, that she was sensitive to my hurt. Brandi continued to stay with me until I decided to moved back to North Dakota, when I had to return her to Brett.

**F.E.A.R.—False Evidence Appearing Real.**
You may have seen this acronym before, but do you understand what it means? The devil is the master at lying and giving us half-truths, which can then appear as a truth. Those thoughts you have in your head such as "I'm not good enough" or "I can't do this" are all from the devil. He likes nothing more than to paralyze you with fear, so you don't walk in the victory God has for you. Speaking these lies to yourself long enough will convince you that they are real, when in fact they are false!

Here are a few scriptures where God warns us about fear and the devil's lies.

> **Proverbs 29:25 (TLB):** *Fear of man is a dangerous trap, but to trust in God means safety.*

> **Isaiah 41:10 (TLB):** *Fear not, for I am with you. Do not be dismayed. I am your God. I will strengthen you; I will help you; I will uphold you with my victorious right hand.*

> **2 Timothy 1:7 (NKJV):** *For God has not given us a spirit of fear, but of power and of love and of a sound mind.*

There are many other scriptures on fear, too many to mention here. You may want to research this subject yourself. Fear is the root of so many harmful emotions. But as you read in 2 Timothy 1:7, God did not give us a spirit of fear.

When you catch yourself feeling fear, in whatever form it may show up, take a deep breath and ask yourself these things: Would I normally have control over this? Why am I so afraid? Will worrying about it change anything? Is there something I can do to snuff out this fear? Is there someone I could go stay with tonight? Don't forget where fear comes from—the devil. DON'T give him that power over your life! Keep in mind the scriptures. The most important weapon you have when fear creeps in is God's Word. Speak scripture out loud, it storms the heavenlies and brings the power of God into the situation!

## Anxiety

A sister to fear is anxiety. They pretty much go hand in hand, with fear being the root of anxiety. I didn't know how I was going to move on past the divorce. You see, I worked for my husband. So now, I not only lost my husband, and was assaulted, but I also lost my job. Could it get any worse? How was I going to make ends meet? What would I do for a job? Where will I live? A couple months had gone by from the time of the attack until I moved back to North Dakota, so I had lots of time to dwell on these negative thoughts. They kept spinning in my head, but with no answers.

Anxiety is fear of the unknown. It is easy to get nervous, apprehensive and tense about something that hasn't even happened yet. And for that matter, may never happen. Worrying is a complete waste of time, because you cannot control the future. You will expend valuable time thinking about something that *may* happen, which in turn steals from you living in the present.

God's word is very clear on this subject. Look at these scriptures:

> **Matthew 6:27 (NIV):** *Can any one of you by worrying add a single hour to your life?*

> **Matthew 6:31-34 (NIV):** *So do not worry, saying 'What shall we eat?' or 'what shall we drink?' or 'What shall we wear?' for the pagans run after all these things, and your heavenly Father*

*knows that you need them. But seek first His kingdom and His righteousness, and all these things will be given to you as well. Therefore, do not worry about tomorrow, for tomorrow will worry about itself. Each day has enough trouble of its own.*

**Philippians 4:6-7 (NIV):** *Do not be anxious about anything, but in every situation, by prayer and petition, with thanksgiving, present your request to God. And the peace of God, which transcends all understanding, will guard your hearts and your minds in Christ Jesus.*

**1 Peter 5:7 (NIV):** *Cast all your anxiety on Him because He cares for you.*

There is a song by Brandon Heath called "Hands of the Healer"[1] from his *Blue Mountain* CD that I love. The words of the chorus are what really ministered to me. In it we are presented with the question of why pray if you are going to continue worrying about it? Prayer implies trusting God with the situation. Worry cancels out your prayer, so if you pray about it, leave it in His hands! Worry is also the opposite of peace. You may want to look up this song and let it minister to you.

When feeling anxious, take a breath and remind yourself that these negative thoughts will *not* solve anything. Focus on anything positive that you can think of, no matter how small. Give thanks for that positive thing in your life and take one day at a time.

> **Philippians 4:8 (NKJV):** *Finally, brethren, whatever things are true, whatever things are noble, whatever things are just, whatever things are pure, whatever things are lovely, whatever things are of good report, if there is any virtue and if there is anything praiseworthy—meditate on these things.*

We all have something to be thankful for. It may not feel like it when you are enduring a traumatic time in your life. But consider these things: Do you have a roof over your head, food to eat, and clothing? How about hot water for a shower? Do you have a close friend or family member who supports you? Are you able to pay your bills, even if things are tight? The fact that you are able to read this book is a blessing, some can't read. As

Philippians 4:8 emphasizes, *whatever* you can think of, no matter how small, give thanks for it. Again, turn to God's holy scripture for help.

## Betrayal

Have you ever trusted someone: a family member, friend, pastor, co-worker or neighbor and then they did something that took that trust away? I'm guessing you felt betrayed. If you have ever had someone cheat on you, steal your idea, manipulate you, or lie to you, then you have experienced betrayal. Trusting that person again can be very difficult. This is what happened to me when I found out Brett was having an affair. It is a gut-wrenching feeling. The person who betrayed you will have to *earn* your trust back, if you are willing to do that. If you recall, this is the very reason our pastor told Brett he had to be accountable to me.

Being betrayed is not something you can control. However, how you react to it is in your control. Will you choose a positive approach or a negative one?

A negative approach will bring on a pity party, feeling anger and possibly even a focus on revenge. When you dwell on the negative, it is like a fast-growing parasite. I recall something my pastor told me. He said, "Sin breeds sin." Think about it, isn't that the truth? One lie can turn into two, then three and so on. Then you can find yourself needing to protect that lie, so then you resort to more drastic measures. All of which are one sin on top of another. That statement has always stuck with me.

Positive responses are intentional, tough choices to make when you are in the midst of a hurt. However, the payoff is worth the struggle. Perhaps you can do something kind for someone else. Blessing others is a powerful weapon against self-pity and other negative emotions. Being intentional puts power back into *your* hands, rather than emotions having the power over you.

## Anger

Oh, how I was so angry at Brett for betraying me! And I was angry at his mistress. The thought of her made me livid. I probably even hated her, even though I knew I should never hate anyone. She showed up at our church one Sunday and looked our pastor in the eyes and said that my husband would be hers one day. I still can't believe she did that! Needless to say, I think most of my anger was directed at her.

Anger that is not dealt with will lead to bitterness. Be very careful not to hold on to anger. It is a natural response, but you must be aware of it and nip it in the bud before it grows out of control.

Often anger is directed towards God. Have you ever asked God the question, "How could you let this happen?" or "What kind of loving God would allow this?" Often people will blame God when something bad happens but fail to give Him credit when they are blessed. And it seems the devil is forgotten about. It is important to understand that God gives us free will to make our own decisions. Many of the problems we face in life are due to poor decisions we make or those that others make. God did not tell someone to fly a plane into a building, that was their choice. He did not tell a drunk driver to get behind the wheel of a car, that was their decision. These things are not God's doing.

**John 10:10 (NKJV):** *The thief does not come except to steal and to kill and to destroy. I have come that they may have life and that they may have it more abundantly.*

We see in this scripture that the devil is on a mission to mess up your life. God is on a mission to save you, bless you and He loves you unconditionally. The Bible gives us fair warning that we will suffer tribulation in our lifetime. Try to avoid the trap of blaming God. He is not your enemy.

**John 16:33 (ESV):** *I have said these things to you, that in me you may have peace. In the world you will have tribulation. But take heart; I have overcome the world.*

## Hatred

This is something I have rarely felt throughout my life, but I felt it towards Brett's mistress. I think what set me off with her was when she kept pursuing Brett after he broke it off. And then again when she showed up at our church. I could not grasp that someone would be so devious and manipulative. I knew my feelings towards her were wrong, but they were hard to shake.

If it weren't for my relationship with the Lord, that hatred would have taken over my heart and made me a very bitter person. This could have caused me to do something I would have regretted. But I did not want to hold on to it, so I asked God to help me let it go. Hatred will destroy you from the inside out. Holding on to hatred gives power to the other person, as well as the devil to keep you in bondage.

Suffering a traumatic event in your life at the hands of another person can cause hatred to grow in your heart. It is understandable, as in my case, but it doesn't make it right. So, you must address the feelings of hatred immediately before it grows out of control.

But sometimes I see hatred so strong in a person's heart for no valid reason. This seems to be most prevalent when it comes to religious differences, race issues, and politics. Instead of agreeing to disagree on the subject, hatred develops for a person. You cannot allow yourself to hate someone just because they have a different viewpoint. It does not mean they are a bad person, they just have different views. Maybe their view is not in line with God's ways, but we are to hate sin, not the sinner.

If you feel hatred in your heart towards anyone, please give it up now! Ask God to help you. Ask every day until you have let it go. Pray for the person, it will help break that bond of hate. Yes, I said pray for them. I had to do this. It was not easy praying for those that hurt me, but necessary and effective. Look at it this way, how messed up must their life must be for them to be able to hurt you so deeply. They don't need your hatred, they need God. Now is an opportunity to intercede for them. The more you practice this, the more the hatred will start to melt away.

> **Matthew 5:44-45 (NKJV):** *But I say to you, love your enemies, bless those who curse you, do good to those who hate you, and pray for those who spitefully use you and persecute you, that you may be sons of your Father in heaven.*
>
> **Proverbs 10:12 (NKJV):** *Hatred stirs up strife, but love covers all sin.*

## Shame/Embarrassment

The feeling of shame or embarrassment is so prevalent among abuse and rape survivors. It can even be emphasized by others who don't understand what it is like to go through these things. If you have experienced a trauma like this, please know it is *not* your fault. You have *nothing* to be ashamed of. The person(s) who did this to you is the one at fault. You may have been in a very vulnerable state and taken advantage of because of it. Someone else made the decision to hurt you. I have experienced this shame and sometimes it tries to creep back in, but I won't let it!

Shame is a slippery slope that can lead to depression. The devil likes nothing better than to hold you captive in shame, or in any of these negative feelings. He wants you to stay victimized and paralyzed by these unhealthy emotions. Knowing this ploy is of the devil can arm you with power to combat these attacks.

Embarrassment could have held me back from publishing this book. However, I refuse to let that creep back in to my life and hold me hostage. Any time you expose the devils lies, it breaks the bondage it has over you.

This has been a very humbling process that has blessed me along the way. Don't be afraid to share your story. Starting with just one person helps the healing process. Keeping everything bottled up inside, keeping it a secret, plays into the enemy's hands. Suppressing the hurt will eventually grow into deeper wounds.

## Failure

Have you ever had something go terribly wrong? Did you feel responsible? Were you quick to label yourself a failure? Unfortunately, this is all too common and how I felt, but it is a lie! You are *not* a failure! Bad things happen, it is a part of life. I've heard an expression along the lines of "failure is a new opportunity." Meaning, it is a chance to learn from the experience by examining what went wrong.

If you fail when attempting to do something it means your actions or decision failed. It does not mean *you* are a failure. Those are two different things. Labeling yourself a failure starts to define you as a person and takes away your value. We all have value, but all have failed in some manner. Scripture says this:

**Romans 3:23-24 (NKJV):** *For all have sinned and fall short of the glory of God, being justified freely by His grace through the redemption that is in Christ Jesus.*

When you make wrong choices in life, you have one of two routes you can go down. First, you can choose to label yourself as a failure, and allow other negative emotions to set in. Over time, you will see your life begin to shatter, causing your spirit to break. In a sense you are convicting yourself for not being perfect. But you need to remember, *no one* is perfect. There is not a person alive that has not made a mistake, so you are in good company! In fact, Jesus addresses this issue when the scribes and Pharisees brought to Him a woman who was caught in adultery. At first glance this scripture may sound harsh towards the woman. However, once you understand he was making a point to the accusers, it was quite genius.

**John 8:7 (NKJV):** *He raised Himself up and said to them, "He who is without sin among you, let him throw a stone at her first."*

The second option you have is to choose to learn from that mistake. Take some time and evaluate what happened. What can you do to avoid the same type of situation in the future? Did you know there are several products on the market today that started off as a mistake and not the intended result? But it was discovered that mistake had great value. Think of failures as open doors for something better. Regain control before your emotions start to dictate your life. And if they already have, then now is a good time to start taking back that power.

Embrace the new opportunity set before you and stop calling yourself a failure!

## Other Types Of Hurts

There are endless ways that pain can be inflicted upon you. Some of these may include: armed robbery, murder, rape, sexual abuse, physical abuse, betrayal by a friend or family member, being lied to, a co-worker hurting you, being abandoned, threatened, enslaved, or being hurt by a trusted leader. Whatever the hurt may be, it will be followed by some type of feelings. Knowing how to deal with your emotions can save you from additional pain and hopefully shorten the time you need for healing.

How are you feeling up to this point? Did anything I described about the various emotions ring a bell? There are so many more feelings that you may have experienced. Look at the list below and see if any of them resonate with you. If so, please promise yourself that you will address it. Any negative emotion that is left unattended will fester into deeper problems. Nothing good ever comes from embracing these negative feelings. It is natural to experience all of these, but you must make a conscious decision to not let them control you.

## Additional Emotional Responses

Here are a few other emotional responses you may have experienced: feeling judged, frustrated, offended, sad, resentment, insecure, worthless, damaged or violated. Other feelings of paranoia, terror, disappointment, vulnerability, panic, abandonment, dismay, apprehension, nervousness and many more are common. In some cases, phobias may develop as a response to these emotional triggers.

Do any of these describe how you are feeling? The bigger the hurt, the more intense those emotions are, and the longer it will take to heal.

There is hope. You can achieve a life filled with joy again, and I will show you how.

God created emotions in us, but it is up to us to learn when to embrace them and when to let them go. It is not expected to think you will *get over* the hurts overnight. It all depends on what you are going through. The healing process is just that, a process, and it is different for everyone. To *feel* the emotion is not a sin. But it is possible to allow the emotion to cause you to sin. Try to be aware of how you are handling each emotion and act where needed. I will help with this in Chapter 11.

# Chapter 3
# Too Good to Be True?

Shortly after Brett and I divorced, I was starting a new life back in North Dakota, my home state. I love that state; their winters may be long and cold, but it has a calmer way of life. After the divorce I stayed in touch with Brett's parents and sisters, occasionally making trips back to visit. During these visits I also got to know his sister's pastor, Greg. On one of those visits he tried setting me up with a guy from his church, Jerry. I fought God on this all the way on my drive home that weekend. Finally, I said, "Fine!" But I'm not sure I believed anything would come of it because of the distance. We lived almost 400 miles apart.

On one of his scheduled visits we were going to a Neil Diamond concert, one of my favorite singers. Before Jerry arrived, a thought popped into my head, one that I thought might be from

God. But I quickly began arguing with God that I could not do it.

Neil Diamond did not disappoint that night, it was a great concert. When we got home, Jerry was excited to share a surprise he had for me. He turned off all the lights and then there was a small light that came on. That light came from a small box that shined brightly on a beautiful heart-shaped diamond ring that sparkled in the light. He proposed! That was the very thing I told God I couldn't do, it was too soon. Yet I found myself saying yes. I think I was both excited and scared at the same time. But it felt so good to find love again.

Life was looking up. Jerry was such a great guy, a Christian who loved the Lord. He treated me so well, and we were in love. Jerry was also a singer and played guitar. I remember one time when I came home from work and checked my messages on the answering machine. There on the machine was a message from Jerry, but not just any message, it was a song that he wrote and sang for me. What woman wouldn't love that? I felt like I struck gold!

We were married in the fall of 1996 on a beautiful, warm, sunny day. I felt like a model in my beaded wedding dress, hair and makeup perfect, driving my friend's convertible. My family made the long trip for the wedding, so all the people I loved were there. Our pastor was feeling proud of himself for setting us up. Ok, I had to give him that one, I was blessed. God was shining down on us!

We settled into our new life together in a quaint river town. Jerry bought the business he had been working for and I found a good job at a real estate office. I was feeling so blessed and thankful to God for restoring joy to my life.

I recall Pastor Greg saying on our wedding day that God was a God of restoration. That is so true. Scripture supports this belief as well.

> **Psalms 23:3 (NKJV):** *He restores my soul; He leads me in the paths of righteousness for His name's sake.*

> **Isaiah 38:16 (NKJV):** *O Lord, by these things men live; and in all these things is the life of my spirit; so you will restore me and make me live.*

**Isaiah 57:18 (NKJV):** *I have seen his ways, and will heal him; I will also lead him, and restore comforts to him and to his mourners.*

Over the course of the next few years, we moved into our cozy little home and were enjoying life. Eventually Jerry decided to downsize the business and move it into the basement of our home. I took over the business and Jerry found a different job.

## Moving On

Late in the year 2000, Pastor Greg and his family moved back to their home state of Illinois to pastor a church. Shortly before they left there was a visitor to our church, whose name was Kyle. He continued to come to church after the pastor moved away. I wasn't quite sure what to think of him, but we tried to make him feel welcomed.

The associate pastor, Dave, was voted in as the head pastor of the church. I think he may have been a bit nervous, who wouldn't be their first time pastoring a church. He met with the men of the church weekly on Friday mornings for prayer. One thing they had prayed for was for

God to send Pastor Dave a mentor. Upon meeting Kyle, they felt he could be the answer to their prayers. Kyle joined the men in prayer those Friday mornings and spent time with Pastor Dave.

After a few short months, Pastor Dave apparently felt Kyle was not a good fit and did not want him involved with the church. I believe Kyle was being a bit too controlling and wanting more power. But I can't say for sure what happened or what was said during those months, as I was not involved in those conversations. Jerry privately kept meeting with Kyle, apart from the Friday morning prayer time as he felt like he was learning so much from Kyle.

Prior to this, for months after the former pastor left, Jerry and I were feeling like we didn't quite fit into our church. We didn't have issue with anyone, it may have been more insecurity than anything. Others had left the church for various reasons, but that didn't play into our decision either. We were questioning, if we were to find another church, where would we go? There were not a lot of options and the one we thought would be the best fit, still wasn't what we wanted. I was feeling unsettled.

At some point, Kyle told Jerry he was planning on planting a new church in the area and invited us to attend. Since we had already been questioning whether we should be looking for a new church, we decided in May 2001 to make the move to Kyle's church. I was a bit reluctant to make the move but was willing to give it a try. We were told not to talk to people from our other church, as they were negative and saying bad things, and would try to influence our decision. That made me a bit uncomfortable, but it seems the separation kept us apart anyway.

## The New "Church"

At first, we were meeting in homes, as Kyle did not have a building yet. It was similar to small groups that meet in homes for Bible study. But the more I was around Kyle, the more I "raised an eyebrow." Unfortunately, it didn't take long before I decided I did not like Kyle. He had a very strong personality, a bit rough around the edges and hard for me to like. I don't always handle strong personalities well, so I figured I was just being silly and needed to be more accepting. After all, my husband had accepted Kyle and enjoyed being with him. Jerry did admit at first, he struggled with Kyle's personality, but grew to accept it, and told me to give him time.

I can't say that there was ever a time where I felt like I was "warming" up to Kyle. He was disrespectful of our time, very demanding and controlling. I kept thinking eventually Jerry would see through this as well. Here's one example of that.

The weekend was approaching, and we wanted to go camping. There was a county park that we loved because it was so peaceful, and we tried to camp there at least once a year. When we mentioned to Kyle that we had planned a camping trip, he was not a happy camper (pun intended). He tried to talk us out of it. And one of his arguments was very telling of something deeper within.

It was supposed to be about 100-degree temps that weekend, with high humidity. Kyle, in his feeble attempt to stop us from going, said, "OK, but don't be surprised if God makes you stay in that hot tent praying all day." What?!! The loving God I serve would never do something like that. What he was describing was a cruel god. My God, Jesus Christ, is a loving, compassionate God. He created the nature that we were going to spend the weekend enjoying. Why would he keep us from that? Kyle continued to give me ammunition to dislike him more and more!

Despite the opposition, we packed up and went camping that weekend. For me, it was probably the most relaxing, blessed weekend of camping I have ever had. We spent time on the lake floating around, swimming, and taking in all of God's beautiful creation. Because it was so hot, we were in the water much of the time, not in a hot tent! I think God went out of his way to bless us and show us He was nothing like the cruel god that Kyle was describing.

> **Ephesians 3:20 (NKJV):** *Now to Him who is able to do exceedingly abundantly above all that we ask or think, according to the power that works in us.*

With the temperature being so hot that weekend, I was concerned how fun camping would be. Not because I was worried God would make me stay in the tent and pray, I knew that was a farce. But when it is nearly 100 degrees, it can be miserable to be outside. But the scripture above jumped off the page of the Bible into my life that weekend. Praise God indeed!

One thing did give me cause for concern on that camping trip. I tried talking to Jerry about how I did not care for Kyle, using his opposition to us camping as an example. Jerry defended Kyle and told me I was overreacting and made some excuse for why Kyle may have acted that way. I was perplexed. How could Jerry be so blinded when it came to Kyle? I wanted to sever the relationship with Kyle, but I simply could not get through to my husband.

I was thankful for a wonderful weekend but knew who was waiting back home for us. I didn't want to go home. Surely something would grab Jerry and wake him up to see what was really going on with Kyle. I had to make Jerry see the truth, but how? I kept hanging on to hope.

# Chapter 4
# The Beginning of the End

It was a beautiful summer Saturday afternoon with the sun shining brightly. I was in the garden pulling weeds and Jerry was working in the garage. Any excuse to be outside in the summer makes me happy! Then we had an unexpected visitor, Kyle. He wanted us to drop everything and come in the house. What was up? He was quite persistent, so I thought it must be something serious. Turns out it was nothing, he just wanted to control us, making us stay in the house and listen to him flap his lips. Reflecting on this, I think he was jealous of Jerry and I enjoying life together. That afternoon did not sit well with me. It took every bit of self-control I had to bite my tongue.

When we met at Kyle's house for church Sundays, I felt like I was in prison. In his attempts to control us, he would talk for hours, mostly about nothing important. He was totally content sitting on his keister for hours on end, but this fidgety girl just about exploded every time. If you are someone who has a hard time sitting still, or has restless leg syndrome, like I do, then you know exactly what I am talking about. I was stuck there, and I came to dread Sundays. Miserable doesn't adequately describe how I felt, and I couldn't understand why Jerry was so enthralled by this guy. To gain back control of a tiny portion of my life, I suggested we always have church at our house. At least that way I was in my own domain. Much to my surprise Kyle agreed.

To compound being miserable, I was having a lot of issues with dry eyes during this time. My eyes would sting and hurt so bad that it was hard to keep them open. On one of these lengthy Sundays I was pinching my eyes closed, as I often did when they were hurting. I got accused of being disinterested and not caring about God's Word. Truth be told I was disinterested, not in God's Word, but in hearing this man's voice for hours on end. This was probably the only time my husband stood up for me and explained why I was acting as I was. But Kyle did not apologize.

On another Sunday I was starting to get a migraine, so I decided to put myself first. After listening to Kyle talk for hours, I got up (without excusing myself) and went and laid down on the bed. He was furious with me when he finally realized I was not coming back in the room. At this point I really didn't care what Kyle thought. I was so fed up with him.

About now you are asking yourself, "Why did we keep meeting with this guy?" That is a fair question. I wanted to run as fast as I could from Kyle, but Jerry was being sucked in. I clung to hope that Jerry would see what I saw, so I was waiting on him. I needed to save my husband. And the longer I stayed the harder it was to leave.

The more I tried to talk to Jerry about Kyle, the more upset he got with me. I am quite certain by this point that Jerry told *everything* we talked about to Kyle and was being coached on how to "handle" me.

During our time of knowing Kyle he had met and married a girl, Lori, almost 30 years younger than him. She had been dating a young man her age, but somehow Kyle managed to convince them that she was meant to be *his* wife. And believe it or not this young man continued to attend his church. But I came to learn rather quickly that his wife was a little mini Kyle. She was calculating, self-absorbed and showed me no respect. In fact, I would catch her flirting with my husband, in front of me. Now I had a double-whammy of arrogance to deal with from these two!

Little by little I watched my husband slip away from me. His emotional departure from me escalated quickly. He was meeting with Kyle more frequently and for longer periods of time. Sometimes he would leave Saturday morning and not come back until almost the next morning. At the time we only had one car, so now I felt like a prisoner in my own home because I couldn't go anywhere. When Jerry was on the phone with Kyle, he would go in the den and shut the door, so I couldn't hear their conversation. Everything started to become a secret, and I was the odd man out.

The stress of all this was taking its toll on me. I couldn't eat much of anything anymore. When I did eat it made me sick. I probably lost about ten pounds. I was the thinnest I had been since before college, an unhealthy weight at my age. I was sick to my stomach all the time from worry of what they were going to do to me next. I was so knotted up from being tense that I needed to see my chiropractor, but I was not allowed to go.

When night rolled around, I couldn't sleep. I would lay in bed and pray that morning would never come.

## Unsubmissive

The personal attacks against me started to come at a greater pace. I was accused of not being a submissive wife. It became their mission to make my life miserable, by trying to make me submissive. There were a couple of other people in the church that Kyle was quite hard on, but they were smart and left!

Kyle, Lori and Jerry would throw out the following scripture at me, Ephesians 5:22-33 and Colossians 3:18. Like so many others have done, Kyle was twisting the true meaning of these scriptures. He was great at using God's Word as a weapon *against* people, rather than to help people.

What does it mean to be a submissive wife? First let's take a closer look at these scriptures:

> **Eph 5:22-25 (NKJV):** *Wives, submit to your own husbands, as to the Lord. For the husband is head of the wife, as also Christ is head of the church; and*

*He is the Savior of the body. Therefore, just as the church is subject to Christ, so let the wives be to their own husbands in everything. Husbands love your wives, just as Christ also loved the church and gave himself for her...*

**Col 3:18-19 (NKJV):** *Wives, submit to your own husbands, as is fitting in the Lord. Husbands, love your wives and do not be bitter toward them.*

Before I answer the question "What does it mean to be a submissive wife?" let me first talk about the husband. The husband is to *love* his wife as Christ loves the church. Jesus is the head of the church, which is often referred to as His bride. The church is also often referred to as the body. The love of Christ is pure, without malice or any evilness. That is how deeply husbands are to love their wives.

Verse 19 says "And do not be bitter toward them." Husbands are not to hold any resentment or bitterness towards their wives. This would mean husbands should show their wives the utmost respect. Abusive acts such as hitting, slapping, pushing, controlling, or abusive language do not fall under the category of husbands being the head of the wife. Under *no* circumstances does a wife have to submit to such horrible treatment from her husband. These scriptures do not say wives are the "property" of the husband, nor does it say they are slaves.

Let's ask the question again, "How are women supposed to submit to their husbands?" Col 3:18 says "As is fitting in the Lord." If the Lord's love for us is pure and for good, then that is how the wife should love her husband. Submission to her husband should come from a place of respect and love, if being submissive falls within the will of the Father. Meaning, abuse is *not* fitting to the Lord.

The husband is the head of the household, under Christ. So that means the husband must answer to God for all the decisions he makes in the marriage. But husbands and wives are to become one, being in unity with one another.

> **Genesis 2:24 (NASB):** *For this reason a man shall leave his father and his mother and shall be joined to his wife; and they shall become one flesh.*

The two shall make decisions together, as each decision affects each other. But when a decision cannot be agreed upon, then the wife should submit to the husband's decision (remember, he is responsible for answering to God as the head.) So, if that decision is wrong, it is not on the wife, but the husband. However, Col 3:18 again says "As is fitting in the Lord." This means the husband's decision should align with the will of the Lord. If what the husband is doing is completely outside the will of God, the wife does not need to submit, as in the case of abuse.

For instance, if a husband demands his wife watch pornography with him, that is something the Lord would call an abomination. Therefore, the wife should not submit to this. On the other hand, if a husband feels he needs to accept a job transfer in another state, then the wife should submit, if all falls under biblical principles.

Husbands who control their wives, are not loving them as Christ loves the church. Monitoring their wife's every move, interrogating her, hitting her, belittling her, name calling, and any other form of disrespect is not the will of the Lord. These things are not showing love, respect or trust. However, these principles also apply to how the woman should treat her husband.

I wish I had understood these principles before my life got any worse. Unfortunately, I had to learn the hard way.

# The Wrath

In attempts to make me submissive, Jerry, Kyle and Lori started to order me around. I recall one day when Jerry demanded that I write out a check to the church. I am a firm believer in tithing. It is biblical as you can see in these scriptures:

> **Numbers 18:26 (NIV):** *Speak to the Levites and say to them: When you receive from the Israelites the tithe, I give you as your inheritance, you must present a tenth of that tithe as the Lord's offering.*

> **Proverbs 3:9-10 (NKJV):** *Honor the Lord with your possessions, and with the first fruits of all your increase so your barns will be filled with plenty, and your vats will overflow with new wine.*

This situation was a bit different, however. My husband was giving this man/church money left and right, into the thousands. I was strongly opposed to the amount of money he was giving him. We barely made ends meet as it was, and this was putting a financial strain on us.

When he approached me that day, I asked him, "Why do *I* have to write it out? You do it." His response was, "Because I'm telling you to." He knew I was opposed to the amount he was giving, so in his mind, he was trying to make me submissive. Keep in mind he was being brainwashed by Kyle, who was after our money.

This made me furious. It is probably safe to say I hated everything about Kyle. The sight of him made my blood boil. The loving husband I once had was long gone because of this man. He had destroyed our marriage and our finances, not to mention the things he did to me.

Again, you may be asking me, "Why did you stay?" Another valid question. First, I'll start by saying, as I mentioned in Chapter 1, I take my marriage vows very seriously, for better or worse, though I now know abuse is not acceptable. But there is more to it than that. By this time, my self-confidence and self-worth were taken from me and fear had set in. Unless you have been in an abusive situation, it is hard to understand. This was a subtle process over a long period of time to try and break my spirit. When an abuser belittles you, cuts you down, and makes you feel worthless over a length of time, you begin to believe it. This creates insecurity and fear within you. Fear can make a person do something they would not normally do (or not do something, like running). So, I stayed out of fear.

I think it is also important to note that the brain is a very strong, yet sensitive organ. It is the most complicated organ in the body. But the brain is also easily altered by outside influences. In my case, there was a lot of neurochemistry going on because of the abuse. That can cause changes in the way we think and process things. I can't explain the science behind it, but it is a real thing.

Therefore, people in abusive situations don't *just leave* like you think they should. It sounds like a simple decision to make. But in reality, a person suffering abuse is not able to make rational decisions in the same manner as someone who has not suffered abuse. Plus, because the abuse started off gradually, it wasn't as noticeable right away. I compare it to the old adage of boiling the frog. In case you haven't heard it, it goes something like this: If you put a live frog in boiling water, it will jump out. But if the frog is put in cool water and then you slowly turn the heat up, the frog does not perceive the danger and ends up being boiled to death.

In continued attempts to make me *submissive*, they tried something new. Jerry had me pack a bag for an overnight trip. I thought we were going somewhere together, though I didn't want to go with him. And he wouldn't tell me where we were going. I was confused because this was on a Sunday, and he had to work the next day. I figured he must have taken a day off. Once in the car Jerry told me he was taking me to a hotel (in one of our favorite cities) and was going to leave me there. Yes, leave me there alone, with no transportation until I was picked up again. He told me I was to think about what it meant to be a submissive wife. It was a long, very quiet drive. I was furious, smoke was probably billowing from my ears! What was I supposed to do for food, there was nothing next to the hotel? Oh, I could walk down the road, then cross the 4-lane highway to go to the truck stop. Right!

After getting checked in to the hotel, Jerry and I walked in the room and was met with a horrible smell. There was no way I could stay in that room. We talked to the front desk and they said they would try to take care of it. So, we decided to go to the park and walk around to kill time. To say the least, that was a very uncomfortable outing. Not sure if I said two words to Jerry that whole time. When we went back to the hotel, the room still smelled bad and I refused to stay there. The hotel did not have another room for me, so Jerry was forced to take me home! To this day I am a bit surprised that he did not try to find another hotel. I think he was a bit flustered that his plan had failed!

The verbal and emotional abuse continued. One holiday, either Thanksgiving or Christmas I was told I could not go back to North Dakota to see my family. They said that I cared "too much" about my family, therefore needed to be taught a lesson. Say what, I cared too much? I've never heard of such a dumb thing. Again, I was livid, and argued with Jerry and Kyle, to no avail. Then it clicked for me. Tell them what they want to hear.

Let the reverse mind games begin! I waited several days before I said anything, but then said to Jerry that I didn't want to see my family anyway, in the condition that I was in. And not long after that I got the news that I could go home for the holiday. Aha! I finally figured them out, at least to a point.

Kyle wasn't through with me yet. He still wanted to control my every move. After all, by now he was already controlling Jerry's every move. So, one day he told me that I could no longer have sex with my husband unless I got permission from him, Kyle, first. Excuse me? No one is telling me when I can and cannot have sex with my husband. Didn't matter though, Jerry and I didn't even sleep in the same room anymore. Our marriage was fast approaching the end. I had even taken off my wedding ring because I did not recognize this man I was living with. I had been trying to figure out how I could leave and where I should go. But I was not quick enough, as you will see next.

This next thing is very difficult to say, making myself vulnerable to all of you reading this. But it is an important piece of the story. At one point, Kyle then sexually assaulted me. After the fact I found out something equally as sad, and that is Jerry knew about it, and purposely left me alone with Kyle. I felt like I was married to a pimp, and he just sold me for the "praise" he would get from Kyle for being obedient. This was their ultimate, final attempt to make me submissive. How twisted can a person be to do this?

Talking about this time of my life is so much more difficult than the story in Chapter 1. Can there be a more hurtful betrayal of a husband? Emotionally I was spent, with no more fight left in me, I felt completely defeated. Any shred of hope that I may have held on to was now gone. This sealed the deal to the end of our marriage. To this day it is hard to admit that I stayed in this relationship so long that it led to the unthinkable. Even though I understand more about how the grip of fear can affect a person's life, and alter their mind, I wish I could have mustered up the courage to leave sooner.

I was distraught and wished I wasn't alive. Thankfully I had a relationship with Jesus and knew that was not the answer. Suicide was never a serious consideration. Then the thought came to me to test Jerry to see if he had a spark of compassion left in his heart. Due to some sleep issues I had a prescription for sleeping pills. I took a couple of pills, then set the bottle on the bedside table. Then I grabbed a piece of paper and wrote out a suicide note. I slid the note under his bedroom door (remember we were no longer sleeping together). This was a cruel thing to do, I know. But I was desperate to see if there was any hope of saving my husband.

The next morning, I was lying in bed awake, but with my back to the door. I heard Jerry quietly come in, so I laid still pretending to be asleep. Jerry could tell that I was breathing and left the room. He did not come running into the room. He did not shake me to see if I was OK. He also did not ever talk to me about it. Not one time was it brought up. Honestly, I think he was disappointed that I was alive, with me out of the picture it would have made things much more simplified.

Those are some harsh things to say about my husband. Sadly, they are all true. If my spirit wasn't already crushed, it was completely crushed that morning. I do not recommend anyone doing what I did. It is a very tragic subject, and one not to be played with, but it is where my mind went at the time. In my heart I knew there was no saving Jerry before this ever took place. Yet in my desperation, this is what I did. Please do not judge me for this, keep in mind, I was not in my right mind at the time.

Now I had to figure out how to get out of that house, out of the marriage. This was not going to be an easy task. What came next was another battle.

# Chapter 5
# Relentless!

True to his secretive life, I overheard Jerry on the phone in the basement talking to Kyle. Yes, I did eavesdrop, I had to know what they were cooking up next. Kyle told Jerry to drop me off at a hotel that night, then the next day load up my possessions and put them in a storage unit. I could not believe my ears. I needed to get out of there fast! I was not about to be stranded at a hotel. Keep in mind, we only had one vehicle.

I grabbed the car keys and headed out the door. Unfortunately, Jerry heard me leave and came running after me. He yanked me back as I was trying to get in the car, asking me where I thought I was going. I told him I wanted to go for a drive to think. Jerry said no I wasn't, he was taking me to a hotel and moving me out the next day. We argued, I told him he couldn't do that, it is my house too. He said, "No it isn't, my name is the one on the deed." I derailed his argument when I reminded him that we refinanced and at that time added my name to the deed. He still insisted that he was moving me out.

Jerry kept pulling on my arm as I was trying to get away from him. Finally, I did something I have never done before, I gave him a knee to the groin. It wasn't with a lot of force, but enough to make him lose his grip. As I was trying to get into the car a second time, he again grabbed me. I felt I had no choice but to give him the knee again. This time I was able to drive off.

Where was I going to go? I had no idea, I just drove. Suddenly I realized, I can't go back home, and I only had the clothes on my back. Needing money, I drove to the ATM machine to withdraw the daily limit. Then I drove to a store to shop for some basics such as a toothbrush, toothpaste, deodorant, and a change of clothes. While shopping, I recalled that a friend's husband that I use to work with was an attorney. But how could I tell her what happened to me? I couldn't, I was so embarrassed.

Instead I called her and told her I had a friend who was going through a nasty divorce and I was trying to help her. She gave me her husband's contact info and said to have my friend call him in the morning. After we hung up, I felt guilty for lying to her. So, I called her back and confessed that it was me, not a friend, who was going through this. Without hesitation, she invited me to come stay at their house, so I accepted her offer. I needed a place to stay that night and was so thankful to feel safe.

The next morning, I spoke with her husband and told him what happened. He advised I get a restraining order against Jerry and then made the arrangements for me to meet with a women's advocate to make that happen. We filed the petition for restraining order with an urgent request. This was on a Friday. The court advised me it could take until Monday if the judge did not have time that day to read my petition and issue the restraining order. My heart sank, All I wanted was to go home.

While I was waiting to hear back on that, I contacted the local police department to see if an officer could escort me home to gather my belongings before Jerry disposed of them. I think the officer was reluctant at first, but he soon realized why I needed him. We walked into the house to find Jerry and Kyle throwing all my belongings into plastic trash bags. They had gathered most of my stuff already. But I wanted to go through the house and make sure I had what I needed and to see what they had done. As I walked into my bedroom, Kyle followed me in there, shooting his mouth off. I yelled for the police officer to get him out of there. I said he has no right to be there, he does not live there, and I wanted him out of my room. The officer ordered Kyle to go out to the kitchen.

As I walked past Jerry in the hallway, I told him that my ex-husband looked like an angel compared to him. What he was doing to me was despicable. The officer then helped me load my vehicle with the bags containing my belongings. I returned to my friend's house and prayed I would hear from the court. Much to my surprise the phone rang, it was the news I needed to hear! The restraining order was issued, and I just needed to make arrangements with the police.

If I recall, the police called to tell me Jerry was not at home and wanted to know if I knew where he could be found. I knew he would be at Kyle's house, so I gave them the address. Not knowing when he would be served and out of the house, I asked the police how I would know when it was safe to return home. They said I could wait at a predetermined local business and they would have an officer drive over to meet me to let me know when I could go home.

When I arrived home, there were five officers in my driveway. They were so helpful and understanding of my situation. I asked how things went with Jerry. He was indeed at Kyle's house, so they had to order him home immediately to pack his essentials. He wanted to take all kinds of things, I guess, but the police hurried him out of the home with a few clothes and essentials. I guess we really do reap what we sow! Before they left, they offered to do extra patrol in my neighborhood. After the officers left, I went in the house and collapsed in agony and wailed all night.

All I ever wanted was for my husband to love me. I never asked for much, I just wanted to be loved. Throughout all of this I so desperately wanted to save my husband, but I failed. At least that is how I saw it. I felt like I was stupid for letting any of this happen and now I was all alone.

## Next Step

What is my next step? My marriage is over, I'm an emotional wreck and not sure how to tell anyone what happened. And now another divorce. I felt like such a failure. Here I was someone who believed in marriage until death do you part, and I was going through a divorce for the second time.

The first thing I needed to do was report to the police that Kyle had sexually assaulted me. The detective took a brief statement but wanted to have a women's advocate present before hearing the full report. It was difficult telling him everything that happened, but I was happy he brought in the advocate.

When things started going bad with Jerry and Kyle, I started to keep a diary. All the details were recorded daily of their activities and attacks against me. The detective asked me to turn that into him as evidence. At one of our meetings, the detective informed me that he ran a background check on Kyle. What he found was astonishing. He said Kyle had the longest rap sheet of anybody he had ever seen. It was approximately sixty some pages long. I wasn't allowed to look at it, but he told me some of the things on it. One of those things was attempted kidnapping. Wow! I was shocked. The detective wanted to put this guy away for what he did to me. He was such an amazing, compassionate detective, I was blessed to have him on my case.

Knowing of Kyle's rap sheet confirmed to me that this man was dangerous. What I had already felt in my heart now became more real to me, that he could have me killed. I told the detective and my friends that if they found me dead one day, Jerry did it, on the orders from Kyle. But at the same time. I told them I didn't even care if he did. I was that distraught. However, I knew that Kyle was extremely cunning and a career criminal. He may have been too clever to have me killed, but not to make my life miserable. This is why I thought Jerry was disappointed to see that I didn't carry out the suicide attempt.

Kyle was relentless! He continued to control Jerry's every move. I found one of Jerry's notebooks filled with notes he had taken. In it he had written that he was not to give me anything, to make things difficult for me and *not* help me out financially. Clearly that was all coming from Kyle. Indeed, this is what Jerry did. We went through a nasty divorce. They managed to drag it out for a year and a half. There was no reason to have a lengthy divorce, we had no children and no assets of great value. It was simply a ploy to destroy me financially.

The judge did not help matters either. When friends found out who the judge was going to be, they warned me about him. They said he had gone through two nasty divorces and was "taken to the cleaners" by his ex-wives, so he hated women. I don't know if any of that was true, but his ruling makes me think there was some shred of truth to it. He basically had us both walk away with what we had. That meant I was left with *all* the debt and no financial support from Jerry. We had been married for 10 years and I was left holding the bag, while he walked away "scott" free. Their plan worked, they destroyed me financially and emotionally. I was drained and distraught.

Going through a time like this is extremely difficult and emotionally draining. But I had amazing friends that were always by my side. Knowing I was going to have to see Jerry in court during the divorce proceedings, I was a bit nervous. My friends offered to go to court to support me. So much so, that one friend's husband even took time off from work to be in court for me one day. You find out who your friends are through a time like this. Guess who was *not* in court? Kyle and his wife did not bother to show up to offer support for Jerry. That should have been very *telling* to Jerry, but it wasn't.

# Prosecuting Kyle

The District Attorney's office met with me to discuss the case against Kyle. They were willing to prosecute but admitted it would be a very difficult case. I told them I would think about it and let them know if I wanted to pursue it. After much prayer I felt like I should let it go. I let the detective know that I had decided not to press charges. Not long after that I ran into the detective outside the DMV office and we talked. He said he wanted me to reconsider my decision about not pressing charges against Kyle. I told him I felt like God wanted me to let Him deal with Kyle. He understood but he said he had hoped he could have at least gotten some monetary settlement for me, he felt I deserved that much. I appreciated his concern. He truly was an upstanding guy who went the extra mile to see justice for me.

One might think that I was yet another woman too afraid to press charges against a criminal. Normally, I am a strong advocate for pressing charges, especially for sexual crimes so that the perpetrator cannot hurt another person. However, in this case I really felt God was telling me to trust Him, and let it go.

As I began the difficult task of rebuilding my life, I couldn't help but pray for Jerry. He was now living in the same house as Kyle and Lori, under their constant watch. My emotions were all over the place. Somedays I wanted to slap him, other days I was crying for him to be saved. I held on to anger towards Jerry for a long time, but I also was sad for him. The more my broken spirit began to heal the more my heart broke for Jerry. He was under such a demonic influence. I kept praying God would open his eyes. Jerry and I both were victims of Kyle's manipulation and devious plan. But we also were not guiltless in how we handled things.

Months passed by after I made the decision to not press charges. Then I received some startling news! Kyle had died of cancer. I was shocked, and relieved at the same time. I did not wish him dead, but I didn't want him hurting another person. Now he couldn't do that anymore! This was not the expected outcome, nor can I explain how God works. All I know is God told me to trust Him. As in the case in Chapter 1, God spared me from having to go through a difficult court case. I'm thankful the Lord delivered me from this horrific situation.

# Chapter 6
# Who Can I Trust?

Anytime you go through a hurtful experience, it is nice to have someone you can trust to confide in, but sometimes it is hard to trust anyone again. Often, we feel like we are alone, with nowhere to go and no one to turn to. But that is not accurate. You may have to search a little bit, but there is always someone, someplace that you can go to get help. I want to explore with you some of the ways I was, or was not, supported through these situations.

## Family and Friends

Now I was faced with the question of how do I tell my family about all of this? After the attack mentioned in Chapter 1, I told my family what happened. However, the situation with Jerry and Kyle was a bit different. I could not bring myself to tell my parents about the sexual assault. So, they only knew that Jerry became abusive. Therefore, I didn't tell my siblings about it either. This book has prompted me to talk to them and give them an advanced copy, so they can read the story before anyone else. What I went through is not a subject I care to talk about. But God was telling me it was time to tell my story so that others could benefit.

The Lord blessed me with a wonderful family. When it was time for me to move back to North Dakota after Brett and I separated, two of my brothers took time off work, drove over 500 miles one way, and on my brother's birthday to help me. I rented a moving van and we drove through snowy, windy weather most of the way to North Dakota, in very cold temperatures. When we arrived at my new home, my sister and her family were there waiting for us, with a hot, home-cooked meal. We set the table up first, so we could sit down and enjoy that delicious meal. Then we unloaded the rest of the truck. I couldn't ask for a better family!

Unfortunately, not everyone is as blessed as I am to have a great relationship with their family. Or perhaps they don't have much family. If that is you, then I hope you have a few close friends that are there for you. In both of my situations, I also had very supportive, caring friends.

When you go through a difficult period in your life, friends can be like angels. In both of my stories, I relied heavily on my friends, as my family did not live near me. I had the best neighbors, who are still like family to me. They, along with other friends, invited me to join them in family gatherings, holidays, birthdays, etc. They made me a part of their families, which was such a blessing. I don't think I could have survived without them. Having a support system where I was became crucial.

## Women's Shelter

I decided to seek out a support group at the local Women's Shelter after Jerry and I separated. After all, the women there likely suffered some abuse themselves and would be able to relate on some level. The day came to attend the first group session, and I was so apprehensive. I am a very private person, so this was a huge leap out of my comfort zone. Yet I was hopeful to receive some help.

As the session started, the counselor went around the room asking each woman, who had been there previously, how things had gone since the last session. Sure enough, they all suffered from abuse, none like mine, but still abuse. As I listened to each tell their story, I waited for the counselor to interject some words of wisdom. But she didn't. It was more of a finger-pointing session. All I heard was women complaining about the men in their lives.

Leaving there that day I was deeply disappointed in how the counselor handled the session. Maybe I was expecting too much, but I was hoping she would help them see their value, or what choices they may have. I was shocked. Returning for another session was not high on my priority list. However, after thinking about it, I decided I had to give it at least one more try. The following week, I reluctantly went to another session. We had the same counselor and unfortunately nothing changed. It was more of the same complaining, but with no action taken. It took everything within me to not say something to these women. I wanted to blurt out that they don't have to stay in these abusive relationships. I had so much to say, but I knew it wasn't my place to do so. After that day, I never returned; they had nothing to offer me.

Although my experience with a Women's Shelter was not a good one, this does not mean they are all this way. A different counselor may have made all the difference. Or perhaps I should have given it more time. I urge you to consider reaching out to a shelter if they have support groups. I did not have to live there to participate in the group. If there is no Women's Shelter, see if there are any other support groups in the area.

## Churches

At the time of our separation, my sole source of income was from the business that I took over from Jerry. I had some big projects coming up that Jerry was going to do, because I physically could not. What was I going to do now, who could help me? There was a guy that worked for Jerry before he downsized the business. I decided to reach out to him, but I did not know his contact information. Thankfully I knew his sister, Ann, who attended the church that Jerry and I used to attend. I was reluctant to reach out to her, considering the circumstances, but I needed the help. She and her husband, Todd, were so compassionate, and helped me to connect with Ann's brother. Though I didn't give them much detail, Todd asked if he could tell

Pastor Dave. I was hesitant at first but agreed to it.

It wasn't long after I received a call from Pastor Dave's wife, Pam. Again, there was no condemnation, only love. She invited me to come to church on Sunday, but I was not ready for that. Several people from the church were going to be gathering at the church for a work-day to do repairs and clean up around the building. She suggested I stop over to say hi to some old friends, being a more casual setting. I said no at first, I couldn't bear to see anyone. I was so ashamed of what happened. But she kept insisting, telling me none of the people would judge me, but would love on me. Finally, I conceded and did show up that day. As Pam promised, I was met with open arms, hugs and so much love. I gave a huge sigh of relief, and felt a little weight lift off my shoulders. It still took weeks before I had the courage to attend church again.

As I started to attend church, it was not without much trepidation. Not because of the people, they had already proved they loved me and were not judging me. Instead, it was because of the Word of God. What? Let me explain. Kyle, in his attempts to make me submissive would condemn me frequently, by using the Word of God as a weapon *against* me. As I mentioned in Chapter 4, he would throw scripture at me to try and guilt me, name call and scare me. That is not how scripture is meant to be used. Because of this, when any of the scriptures that Kyle used against me were mentioned in church, it made me cringe. It felt like I was punched in the gut at the sound of those words. These scriptures related to a negative time in my life, which stirred up bad memories. God's Word should never make a person feel bad. But I also felt guilty for not wanting to hear these verses. This was something I struggled with for a long time.

There had to be something I could do to get over this "punched-in-the-gut" feeling. The Lord laid it on my heart to recite the very scriptures out loud, that I had trouble hearing. Wow! How could He ask such a thing? It is called facing your fears. Plus, the power of the spoken Holy Word can destroy the works of the enemy. Think about it, if the devil can get you to stay clear of God's Word, then he has won a huge battle. We are fed and strengthened by God's Word, something the enemy does not want to happen.

This was a bold move, but one I had to make. I started to speak those very scriptures that had been used against me. I'm not going to lie, it hurt at first. However, the more I heard myself speak them, the more they began to bless me. The devil cannot stand hearing the Word of God, and he was losing ground every time I spoke. The Lord may ask a difficult thing of you, but it will always be for your own good.

Todd was like a brother to me, and he wanted to see me smile again. He decided to ask me, "Are you happy?" every time he saw me. And every time I told him NO! Todd was persistent, he said he would keep asking until one day I could say yes. I didn't think that day was possible.

Months had gone by when one afternoon I was standing in front of my kitchen sink, doing dishes. Nothing eventful had taken place that day or any other recent day. Then out of nowhere I spoke the words, "I'm happy." I startled myself. Where did that come from? I looked around, as if someone else was in the house with me, even though I knew that wasn't the case. How could I say such a thing? And then I repeated it. Yes, I really felt like I was happy. It came out of the blue, but it was genuine. I guess God had been healing me from the inside out, and it finally struck me. I could not wait to go to church the next Sunday. I walked up to Todd and said,

"Guess what Todd, I'm happy!" If you could have seen the smile on his face. It was priceless. It brought him joy when he heard those two words, and it brought me joy to finally be able to tell him what he waited so long to hear. It even brings tears to my eyes now as I write this. I don't get to see Todd anymore, as we don't live in the same state, but he is dear to my heart, as is his wonderful wife.

Don't discount the idea of reaching out to old friends. You might be surprised at how much they love you and want to support you. Also, don't rule out reaching out to a church. If you don't have a church you attend, find one. Ask to meet with the pastor and find out their beliefs. If you feel comfortable, share what you have gone through. The church you attend should feel like "home." Not all churches are created equal. You may have to search to find that one that gives you a sense of peace, and that "at home" feeling. I suggest praying about it, ask God to lead you to the right church family. It is important that you are fed the Word of God, see growth in yourself, and are able to build relationships. Your church family can be some of your biggest supporters.

Sometimes when we refuse to ask for help, we are actually being prideful. And pride is another form of fear. Don't talk yourself out of asking for help, in whatever form that may be. I wish I had reached out to someone sooner. By not asking for help, we think we are being strong, but that is a misconception. Being able to humble yourself and allow people to help you is actually when you are being strong. It takes a great deal of strength to make yourself vulnerable and allow others to know what has been hidden for so long.

## Ministries Outside of My Church

Three years after Jerry and I were divorced, a co-worker, Val, asked if I wanted to join her in doing a half marathon. At first, I declined, I had never even officially done a 5K, though unofficially I had taken many walks of over 3 miles. Plus, I was not a runner. That did not convince her. Val said she wasn't a runner either, but instead walked it. She encouraged me to give it a try. After some thought I told her, "Oh what the heck, you only live once." However, I had some health issues that made me question my abilities. But I really needed to take this leap of faith and start living life again.

Val and I trained hard for the half marathon. I was more than ready physically, but mentally I was still freaking out. Race day came, no turning back. Val and I reached the 6-mile mark and I said, "We've gone 6 miles already?" Val gave me a dirty look and said "I was thinking, we've *only* gone 6 miles?" That gave me a good laugh! I was having fun, it was a beautiful sunny day in May, and I was so thankful I decided to do this. Up ahead I could see the finish line, how exciting. I did it! I finished my first half marathon. The organizers of the race had a band playing for entertainment at the finish line. I was dancing, as my friends were collapsed on the grass. They looked up at me and asked, "What is wrong with you, you are a freak of nature. We just did a half marathon; how do you have the energy to dance?" I had to laugh again. But the next day I could barely walk!

Fast forward a year, and it was time to sign up for the half marathon again. My thoughts were, piece of cake, last year went smoothly! I got a little too confident and didn't work out quite as hard. Race day came again, but the temps were not as nice. The morning started out in the 40's, which isn't too bad. We dressed a little warmer than the previous year, but not too many layers to avoid getting hot once we started walking. Big mistake! Not long after we left the house a cold front moved in. The temperature quickly dropped to about low 30's and the wind picked up. While we were walking, I recall turning the corner and walking right into the wind. It was gusting so hard that it felt like I was swimming upstream; the wind was pushing me backwards. It went downhill (not the terrain) from there. Crazy is a word that comes to mind, why did I ever sign up to do a second half marathon? I should have quit while I was ahead. As I walked, a thought came to mind, "I need to make some changes in my life". I thought that was pertaining to my physical health as I hadn't trained as hard for this race. My thought was that I needed to exercise on a more regular basis. We all finished that race, but it was another two years before I had the courage to try another one.

A day or two after the race, while I was channel surfing on the TV, I came across Joyce Meyer's program called *Enjoying Everyday Life*.[1] For those that do not know her, Joyce is a Christian inspirational speaker, who often uses her own life experiences as examples. She openly shares about her hurtful childhood which also inspires me to share my story. I had heard her in the past and enjoyed her teachings and found her to be very funny. So, I started watching her program daily. God was feeding me so many nuggets through Joyce Meyer's ministry. Then it struck me: When that thought popped into my head on race day, "I need to make some changes in my life," that it was a message from God. He was trying to tell me I needed to turn to Him, go deeper, and trust Him. It had nothing to do with my physical health but instead my spiritual health. Let's face it, I still had a lot of baggage from my ordeal with Jerry and Kyle.

I tell the race story to encourage you to try something new, get out of your comfort zone. Maybe you feel God is telling you to do something, but you are too scared to do it. Take that leap of faith, I guarantee you will be blessed in the end (and even through the journey).

I also encourage you to broaden your scope of support. There are many good books and ministries that can speak into your heart, as Joyce Meyer did to me. A phrase that Joyce likes to say often, and resonates with me is, "Do it afraid." You can feel afraid, but you don't have to let that fear hold you back. Conquer it, you can do it!

Joyce Meyer has a book called *Battlefield of the Mind, Winning the Battle in Your Mind*.[2] She addresses how our thoughts can affect us and teaches how to renew our minds. This book is a very good resource to have on hand. I highly recommend you read it! You may also want to check out her book *Living Beyond Your Feelings*.[3]

## The Word of God

Last, but not least, is God's Word. In fact, of all these support systems, God's Word is the most critical tool you could use. The Bible is the inspired Word of God. This means that God spoke to everyone that wrote a book in the Bible on what he wanted an account of. In the same manner, God has inspired me to write this book and has helped me to know what to include.

Scripture is meant to edify, teach, correct, encourage, inspire, and give hope to all who hear and read it. Throughout this book I have shared scripture to back up what I was saying. God reveals things in scripture to those who seek it out. You can read the same passage of scripture for years, and then one day it seems a light bulb goes on. He will show you something deeper about that verse. God is multifaceted. He is not limited to one way of speaking to you, nor does he limit His Word to one message. What I mean by that is one scripture can teach you something, and then at another time, God may reveal even more meaning to that scripture. It is like there are layers to passages of scripture, just as you may pull back layers of wallpaper. Each layer is different and reveals a bit more. As you seek to draw closer to God, He will start to peel back those layers and teach you more and more, as you are able to receive it.

If you are new to reading the Bible, it may seem a bit intimidating at first. Where do you start? What should you read? I suggest researching scripture that applies to what you are going through. If you are suffering from fear, then research fear. Once you have found some scriptures, read a few of the verses before and after the verse you chose to help you learn the context in which it was written. You may also want to read from Proverbs daily, consider the Psalms and the Gospels: Matthew, Mark, Luke and John. May I also suggest you consider finding a Bible study group to join or at the very least purchase a beginner's Bible study guide.

Next, choose a few of the scriptures you researched that really *spoke* to you and write them down on a 3x5 index card. Or you may want to print each verse out on a sheet of paper. Then hang them up where you will see them, such as your bathroom mirror, above your desk at home, or even throughout your house. If you can, take a few to work with you.

Each day, multiple times a day, speak those scriptures out loud. I suggest at a minimum speak them when you get up in the morning and before you go to bed at night. The spoken Word is so powerful. As I mentioned before, it is a weapon against the devil. He loses power every time you speak scripture. It also triggers your mind to believe what you say. That is why it is so important to be very careful about anything you speak. Negative thoughts start to become real to you when you speak them.

These steps are things I have practiced through the years and found them to be very helpful. If you are struggling with multiple negative thoughts, it may be easier to find scripture for one at a time. Don't overwhelm yourself with trying to deal with everything at once. You can switch out the verses or add to them as time goes on. Do what works for you.

There are many versions of the Bible, it is a good idea to find one or two that you like the best. Personally, I prefer the New King James Version (NKJV) as my primary Bible. Some Bibles are translated into such modern language that I feel it loses a lot of the impact, but that is just my personal taste. It may also depend on what country you live in or your first language. I have several other versions that I refer to for further clarification. Finding a Bible you like best is a personal decision.

God proved He had a plan when asking me to recite those scriptures out loud. It was to love hearing His Word again and defeat the enemy in this battle. There are many other ways in which God has shown himself to me in the midst of my storms which I will share with you next.

# Chapter 7
# God Winks

Recently I watched a *Hallmark*[1] movie called A *Godwink Christmas*.[2] In it, one of the characters referred to God's nonverbal communication with us as Godwinks, which is where I got my idea for the title of this chapter. The term was coined by Squire D. Rushnell.[3] It is defined as an event or personal experience often described as being a coincidence. With God there are no coincidences! I like the term God wink, because it reminds me of when someone does something nice for you and then you catch them throwing you a wink. It's an act of endearment. It also reminds me of those special moments between you and another person, that only the two of you know about. At times it might cause one of you to wink at the other!

Your heavenly Father loves you unconditionally, and more than you could ever put into words. But sometimes you may not feel Him, or you think He has abandoned you. This simply is not true! Sometimes your circumstances seem so unbearable, that all you can focus on is the negative, and you don't notice the God winks. Scripture tells us that God will never leave us.

> **Hebrews 13:5 (NKJV):** *For He Himself has said, "I will never leave you nor forsake you."*

> **John 14:18 (NKJV):** *I will not leave you orphans; I will come to you.*

Let me share a couple of times that God *winked* at me to let me know that He was still there. I don't recall if this first incident happened while I was still with Jerry or if it was shortly after we were separated. Either way, it was during a time when I was distraught and could not see light at the end of the tunnel.

## Eye of the Hurricane

One sunny afternoon I decided to go for a walk in the woods. Being in nature always makes me feel closer to God because there are no distractions. Listening to birds chirping, squirrels scampering around and leaves rustling in the wind brings a sense of peace to me. While on my walk I talked to God. I shared with him how I was feeling, and I didn't hold back. No need to hold back, as He already knows.

When I came to the trail end at the parking lot, I stopped in the middle of the parking lot and looked up into the bright, blue sky. As the sun was shining down on me, I listened to the trees swaying and leaves fluttering. Suddenly I felt an overwhelming sense of peace and calmness wash over me. The thought that came to mind was that I was in the eye of a hurricane, where it is the calmest. The eye of a hurricane is surrounded by the eyewall, where the most severe weather and highest winds occur. My life was like a hurricane, in complete chaos. Yet in that moment, it was as if there was nothing else around me except overwhelming peace. It let me know that God was still there, looking out for me.

## A Mustard Seed

Another time while still married to Jerry, I was struggling with how much my husband had changed and feared our marriage would end. I knew that I needed to hold on to a mustard seed of faith to get through that time. Scripture states:

**Matthew 17:20 (NKJV):** *So Jesus said to them, "Because of your unbelief; for assuredly, I say to you, if you have faith as a mustard seed, you will say to this mountain, 'Move from here to there,' and it will move; and nothing will be impossible for you."*

I surely had mountains going on in my life that needed to be moved!

Then one day I noticed a tiny spot on the underside of my right wrist, where the hand meets the wrist. I tried washing it off, but it wouldn't come off. It was not there before, so I thought I had developed a freckle. But what struck me was it was as small as a mustard seed. I felt like God had given me a mustard seed mark on my wrist to remind me every time I looked at it that He was with me, and to have faith that he would take care of me.

One evening, Kyle and his wife made plans to go to a movie and wanted Jerry and I to go with them. It was the last thing I wanted to do, but I didn't have a choice. I decided I would hang on to my "mustard seed" while at the movie. When we found our seats, Kyle's wife tried to sit by Jerry, but I foiled those plans and I sat next to her.

Things were not starting off well. I asked Jesus to hold my hand the entire time I sat through the movie. This may sound silly to you, but I needed some comfort. So, I clinched my hand with that mustard seed on it as if I was holding onto the hand of Jesus.

That mustard seed helped me through a very difficult time. I know that it truly was a God wink because after Jerry and I divorced, the mark went away. You can believe what you want, but I choose to believe that God gave me that symbol of faith and hope at a time when I needed it.

What are you going through? Was there a time in your past that was rather difficult? Take a moment and think back, was there ever a time when some small, good thing happened, or you sensed something? Could it be possible that God was winking at you too? Don't discount it. God is not limited to showing Himself to you in ways that only you can think of. He knows what you need, when you need it. And He may surprise you with a God wink when you least expect it, in a way that you could never imagine.

# Chapter 8
# Forgiveness is Not!

Back to the question of how could I forgive the man in Chapter 1? Did I forgive Brett and his girlfriend? Jerry? Kyle? Lori? Forgiving them was a much harder process. The man that broke into my house was basically a stranger, I had met him briefly, but I had no relationship built with him. I didn't like or dislike him, hadn't built up a trust between us, and was not family or friend. It seems to be much easier to forgive a stranger than a trusted family member or friend. In some ways that seems backwards. But when you consider how much you have invested in a loved one, and then they hurt you, that investment seems to have been in vain.

Still, this man violated me and stole my sense of security. Because of what he did, I lived in fear for a long time. He didn't deserve to be forgiven, right? Let's take a closer look at the definition of forgiveness.

Forgiveness is defined as: 1. Pardon, 2. Inclination to forgive; willingness to pardon.[1]

Forgive is defined as: 1. To give up resentment against or the desire to punish; stop being angry with; pardon. 2. To give up all claim to punish or exact penalty for an offense; overlook. 3. To cancel or remit, to show forgiveness.[2]

Whoa, wait a minute! Am I saying all these people should be pardoned, no consequences, no punishment? No, that is not what I am saying.

Unfortunately, too many people misunderstand what forgiveness means. If you take these definitions at face value your initial reaction may be to say, "I can't do that." You may think that person deserves to go to jail, or what they did was wrong and should be punished. Learning what forgiveness is, or is not, will help clear this up.

## Seven Misconceptions of Forgiveness

**First**—We need to understand forgiveness is NOT a feeling. It is NOT an emotion. If we wait to forgive someone until we *feel* like doing it, we will never forgive them.

**Second**—Forgiveness is NOT inaction. The act of forgiving is a choice requiring action, one we can choose to do or not. It is not based on our circumstances, when they are just right, because they will never be "just right". Instead it is a conscious decision choosing to forgive the one who hurt us.

**Third**—Forgiveness is NOT condoning what the person did to you. One of the biggest misconceptions about forgiveness is that by forgiving you are saying what the person did to you was OK. In no way does it mean this. I'd like to share an example of this. After I found out that Brett was cheating on me, and we decided to try to work things out, I chose to forgive him. I had made the comment to a friend, "If God can forgive him, then so can I." What I meant by that was God wouldn't ask me to forgive if He wasn't willing to forgive. That friend repeated it to Brett. I don't know if what I said got twisted or if Brett heard what he wanted to hear. But he went around telling his friends that I was OK with what he did. Finally, someone told me what he was saying so I could set the record straight. Oh, how things get twisted!

Remember the guy in Chapter 1 that broke into my home and assaulted me? I forgave him, but never once did I think it was OK what he did. He committed a terrible crime against me and needed to face consequences, and in this case that meant jail time.

**Fourth**—It is NOT releasing them from their responsibility for their actions, unless we choose to. For instance, if someone owes you money, but they won't or can't pay it back, you could choose to forgive the debt. There is a story in scripture about this:

> **Matthew 18:27 (NKJ):** *Then the master of that servant was moved with compassion, released him, and forgave him the debt.*

You may want to read this whole story, beginning with verse 21. We can release them, but everyone will give an account to God. We are to repent of our sin and our heavenly Father will be faithful to forgive us.

**Fifth**—It does NOT always mean forgetting what happened. Clearly, I have not forgotten the things I went through. If I had, I would not have been able to write this book. But I forgave and now rarely think about those times. And when I do think of them, it is without any bitterness or anger.

When forgiveness is required, it can be for a big or small offense. Think about the times you were cut off in traffic, a sales clerk was rude, or you got into a fight with your spouse or kids. One might classify these as minor hurts. If you remembered every time one of these happened and held on to that offense, think how bogged down you would be. It is possible to forget an event like this whether you chose to forgive or not. That is why it is very important to learn how to forgive quickly so resentment doesn't build up. Don't be discouraged, this is a process to be learned, and a choice you will be faced with as long as you live!

**Sixth**—Forgiveness does NOT always mean you will trust your offender ever again, nor does it mean you *should* trust them. As you just read, I had two ex-husbands that betrayed me. I have forgiven them but doubt I will ever trust them again. I would have to see a total transformation in their lives through Jesus Christ before I would trust them again. Here is another visual to help understand this.

Often an abusive person will say they are "sorry" for what they've done. The person on the receiving end of it, will trust they meant that (at least in the early stages). But then the abuser hurts again and says sorry again. The vicious cycle begins. The victim can choose to forgive the abuser, but to trust that they won't do it again is not to be expected.

This holds true of someone with an addiction. As in the case of abuse, a person with an addiction has an altered mind. Whether the addiction is alcohol, drugs, pornography, or any other addiction, the brain gets "re-wired." This causes the emotional part of the brain to override the reasoning part of the brain. So even though the person may truly desire to do the right thing, their thoughts and decisions become hijacked by the addiction, thus repeating the dangerous behavior. The brain can be restored, but not without proper counseling, which can take years. Relationships can be restored from the hurt of addiction, so do not be too quick to give up on your loved one. You will see an example of this in Chapter 10.

**Seventh**—Forgiveness does NOT mean you will never have more hurts in your life again. In fact, the Bible tells us we will have troubles in life. But by turning to God we can get through those trials with much more grace and peace knowing He will see you through.

**1 Peter 5:10 (ESV):** *And after you have suffered a little while, the God of all grace, who has called you to his eternal glory in Christ, will himself restore, confirm, strengthen, and establish you.*

**John 16:33 (ESV):** *I have said these things to you, that in me you may have peace. In the world you will have tribulation. But take heart; I have overcome the world.*

The act of forgiveness comes from our heart, when we realize it is what is best for us. It is a conscious decision to release that person from your feelings. Forgiveness was defined, at the beginning of this chapter, as giving up resentment, to stop being angry. When you hold on to anger, bitterness, vengeance and so many other negative emotions, you are hurting yourself. Often, the other person doesn't even know that you are harboring those feelings. You are not "hurting them back" by refusing to forgive. So what does it mean to give up all claim to punish, to pardon or overlook? Look at this scripture:

**Romans 12:19 (NKJV):** *Beloved, do not avenge yourselves, but rather give place to wrath; for it is written, "Vengeance is Mine, I will repay," says the Lord.*

It is the Lord's place to judge someone and "deal" with them, not yours. Again, I will say this is an opportunity for you to pray for them. The power of prayer releases that grip that unforgiveness has over you.

## The Grip of Unforgiveness

**Ephesians 4:31-32 (NKJV):** *Let all bitterness, wrath, anger, clamor, and evil speaking be put away from you, with all malice. And Be kind to one another, tenderhearted, forgiving one another, even as God in Christ forgave you.*

As we can see in the above scripture, God is telling us that it is important to set aside our feelings and forgive one another. The Bible is filled with scripture about forgiveness. The subject is obviously of great importance to God if he speaks of it so frequently. Here is one more to consider:

**Matthew 6:14-15 (NKJV):** *For if you forgive men their trespasses, your heavenly Father will also forgive you. But if you do not forgive men their trespasses, neither will your Father forgive your trespasses.*

So, what are the consequences of unforgiveness? When you choose not to forgive someone, you are now classifying yourself as the judge and jury. As you read above, that is the Lord's responsibility. You are holding on to that person, by holding on to that hurt. As Matthew 6:14-15 says, God is unable to forgive you, if you are not willing to forgive. If someone has hurt you so badly, why do you want to hold on to them? Wouldn't you rather forget them? Forgiveness *releases* you from holding on to that person.

Unforgiveness causes bitterness to grow in your heart. If never dealt with, it grows and spawns more sin in your life. The negative emotions discussed in Chapter 2 start to grow and fester. It can cause you to become short-fused with the people around you. They may not even have done something wrong, but any little thing will set you off.

An overall negative attitude can start to form. With this can come a spirit of being judgmental of others. Criticism starts to come naturally for you, finding something wrong is easy. Have you ever heard the term "Negative Nelly?" This is a person who complains about everything, never happy, and basically is an all-around negative person.

Refusing to forgive will eventually harden your heart. This is *not* a place you want to go. A hardened heart will destroy relationships, pushing everyone away. Before long, you will find yourself alone.

As I was writing this, God gave me a vision of what the grip of unforgiveness looks like. The vision was a hand squeezing a heart with so much force that the heart couldn't pump. The heart no longer worked!

It is important to protect your heart. Not only can you become a cold, mean-hearted person, but you can develop health issues. Choosing to change your attitude is health to your soul, as these scriptures points out:

**Proverbs 17:22 (TLB):** *A cheerful heart does good like medicine, but a broken spirit makes one sick.*

**Proverbs 15:13 (NKJV):** *A merry heart makes a cheerful countenance, but by sorrow of the heart the spirit is broken.*

Harboring unforgiveness opens the door to the devil to destroy your life. The following scriptures warn us that what we hold in our heart is who we become. So, if you choose to harbor anger, bitterness or any other harmful emotion, that is who you will become.

**James 4:7 (NKJV):** *Therefore submit to God. Resist the devil and he will flee from you.*

**Matthew 12:35 (NKJV):** *A good man out of the good treasure of his heart brings forth good things, and an evil man out of the evil treasure brings forth evil things.*

**Matthew 6:21 (NKJV):** *For where your treasure is, there your heart will be also.*

**Proverbs 23:7 (NKJV):** *For as he thinks in his heart, so is he.*

There is a song called "Break Every Chain,"[3] written by Will Reagan. The lyrics tell us the chains in our life can be broken through the power in the name of Jesus. The song ends with the hope of hearing those chains fall off.

Some of the chains in your life are those negative thoughts and emotions such as fear, anxiety, stress, and unforgiveness. Forgiveness is the key to unlocking those chains.

I encourage you to look up this song and listen to the words. Close your eyes and envision each chain falling off to the floor. Do you hear the clanging of metal as each link hits the floor? Imagine how light your arms feel with those chains gone. If you do this visual exercise of the physical chains dropping off your arms, shoulders and chest, think how great that would feel to be free. Then transfer that to the burdens you carry, the hurts, pain, bitterness and bad memories. Wouldn't it feel great to be free of those chains?

# Death Stands in The Way

When the unimaginable happens to a loved one because of their own reckless actions or by their own choice, the hurt can be unbearable. Perhaps your son was drag racing and lost control of his car and died in the crash. Or you had a daughter that was experimenting with drugs and overdosed. Then there is the unthinkable act of suicide. The questions and guilt that can overcome those left behind can tear families apart. Anger can set in with the question, "How could they do this to me?"

Hurt caused by these types of situations are very real and may require forgiveness. The person may not have hurt you intentionally and is no longer living. However, it may be necessary for you to forgive them to help you with the grief process. Keep in mind, forgiveness is for *you*, and can be done at any time, whether the person is living or not.

Hopefully some of the misconceptions about forgiveness have been cleared up. Now that you know forgiveness is all about your healing, how do you start? The next chapter will walk you through a few steps to get you started.

## Chapter 9
# Choosing Forgiveness

**Deuteronomy 30:19 (NKJV):** *I call heaven and earth as witnesses today against you, that I have set before you life and death, blessing and cursing; therefore choose life, that both you and your descendants may live.*

Choosing forgiveness is choosing life. The Lord lets you make the decision because you have free will. But He desires all of us to choose life. Holding on to unforgiveness slowly kills you from the inside out. Choosing forgiveness is taking back your life!

## Did I Forgive?

You may still be wondering if I have forgiven the people mentioned in this book that have hurt me. I've already mentioned that I forgave my ex-husbands. What about the others? The quick answer is "yes." Before elaborating on the others, let me tell you a bit more about Brett.

Forgiving Brett took a long time, maybe years, I don't recall. I wish I could say that was the end of it. But Brett continued to hurt me over the years. He remarried twice since our divorce and both women did not like that I continued to stay friends with his family. On more than one occasion, Brett told his family they could no longer be friends with me. One school year, I let his niece live with me while she was in college, but that probably made things worse. Each time I was faced with the challenge of not only forgiving Brett, but his wives as well.

Twenty-three years later when Brett's father passed away, I reluctantly attended the funeral. I wasn't sure how I would be received by the family, but my husband encouraged me to go, so I agreed. The family members were all kind to me. But guess who else attended his funeral? Brett's ex-wife, the one he left me for. Believe it or not, Brett, his ex-wife and his current wife each came up to me that day and hugged me! It was an odd encounter as the four of us stood there talking, but one that was healing. An opportunity even presented itself for me to have a moment alone with Brett to confront him on his years of attacks. He apologized and agreed that they were uncalled for. All is forgiven with all three of them. That past is in the past, I have no desire to think about it or hold on to it. That serves me no purpose!

If I had allowed the fears of the unknown to stop me from going, I would not have experienced such a healing moment. Plus, God allowed me to get reconnected with some of Brett's friends that I had not seen since we divorced. It was such a blessed time. What I'm trying to show you is facing your fears can bring about blessings!

Remember in Chapter 5 when I mentioned I was finally able to tell Todd I was happy? I believe that was because I chose to forgive Kyle and Lori. It took me years before I felt like I had forgiven them, to the point where it didn't make my blood boil to talk about them. But it was the desire of my heart to forgive, and God knew that, and I believe God can work with that. I think God understands our hurts and that healing is a process. Because of that, He helped me find joy again, even though I was still hurting. As I said above, I have no desire to hold on to the past hurts.

I have no regrets in marrying Brett or Jerry. Had I known what would happen I would not have married either one. However, they did not set out to do the things they did. One bad choice led to another and eventually down the wrong path. Holding on to regrets is also another trap of the devil. Regrets keep you living in the past, wishing for this or that. Since you can't change the past, it is time to let it go and focus on the here and now and moving forward.

## Everyday Forgiveness

Sometimes we are faced with the challenge of having to forgive daily, as I was in this next example. Not all things are big traumas, but everyday challenges. These sometimes are the hardest to forgive because you are faced with them every day, and they can wear on you. But learning to forgive the daily things will completely transform your life and prepare you for those bigger things that may come up. I wish I could say I was able to forgive daily, but I can say I learned a lot from this time in my life.

After my divorce from Jerry, I had to find a full-time job with benefits, but I continued to work my business from home for a few years. The job I was offered was in a new department, with only three of us. I continued to work in this same department for seven years before leaving. The department grew from three people to approximately 15-20 people. My manager and I were the original two of the department and went through many changes.

I oversaw a large chunk of the reports for the organization. Throughout the years I developed processes, created reports, trained people and so much more. Because of my job duties, it required me to work with upper management and the president of the organization. I've never been one to be impressed by titles. It was my job to work with them. I respected them and their position, but it didn't make me feel more important because I worked with them. Unfortunately, not everyone looks at it that way. I worked with a group of women who were so jealous of my position that they went out of their way to hurt me.

There were many days I went home from work, and even sometimes on my lunch break, and cried. We could have been such a fun team, but instead their jealousy made it unbearable to work there. I used to love my job, but they caused me to hate it. They even started in on another lady and had her in tears. Thankfully I had a wonderful relationship with my boss, and she could see through it all. However, she was unable to do anything about their behavior, which is another story entirely!

One day I blew up at one of the girls and gave her a piece of my mind. But God dealt with me about my actions. It didn't matter what the other girl did, my actions were wrong as well. So, I had to "suck it up" and apologize. I even bought her a gift card to the local coffee shop as a peace offering. I wish I could say it changed things, but it didn't. Things continued to get worse as time went on with all these women, which is why I left.

Forgiving these women was not an easy task. I tried praying for them, but daily attacks made it difficult. It has taken me years to forgive to the point of feeling like it is real. I can only hope that through all these experiences that I have learned to forgive quicker, and not hold on to the hurt for so long.

## Forgiving Yourself

Sometimes it is necessary to forgive yourself to have complete healing. In my case, I realized I had opened some doors to make it possible for Kyle and Jerry to be abusive. Because of that, I had to learn to forgive myself as well. Forgiving yourself gives you permission to not be perfect, because no one is. It also gives you an opportunity to learn, grow, and draw closer to God. Not only did I have to forgive myself, but I had to fight the self-condemning thoughts. Allowing thoughts such as "feeling stupid" is like putting gas on a fire. It will only lead to more condemning thoughts. This is why the Lord tells us to take every thought captive.

> **2 Corinthians 10:5 (NIV):** *We demolish arguments and every pretension that sets itself up against the knowledge of God, and we take captive every thought to make it obedient to Christ.*

## How Do You Forgive?

In summary, what then does it mean to forgive and how do you forgive? Forgiveness is a conscious decision to release yourself from the offender and the negative emotions you have. It is allowing yourself to be free from the bondage of holding on to pain so that you can begin to heal. It is also regaining power over your emotions, stripping the devil of his grip on you. It is a choice that is probably set before you almost every day of your life.

> **Mark 11:25 (NIV):** *And when you stand praying, if you hold anything against anyone, forgive them, so that your Father in heaven may forgive you your sins.*

**Here are a few steps to help you start the process of forgiveness:**

**First**—Make a list of every person you can think of that you may not have forgiven. Write their names down on a sheet of paper.

**Second**—Start by making the choice to forgive each of these people, even if you don't feel like it. Remember, forgiveness is not a feeling. Make it the desire of your heart to want to forgive, even though it is a hard choice.

**Third**—Speak out loud, "I forgive (insert the name of person(s) you need to forgive)." Continue to do this daily or at least a few times a week. Note: this may hurt at first to voice these words, but it gets easier the more you do it.

**Fourth**—Ask God to help you develop forgiveness in your heart. It is not possible to forgive in your own strength, but the Lord will be your strength.

**Fifth**—Ask God to help you let go of the resentment, bitterness, anger and any other harmful emotions that you feel toward this person. Tell Him it is your desire to put an end to these feelings, but you don't know how to do it. Be honest with how you feel, talk to God openly. He already knows your thoughts and is waiting for you to let Him in on the situation.

**Sixth**—Pray for those that have hurt you. Again, this will be hard at first but will get easier over time. Whoever hurt you obviously has issues in their lives that would lead them to cause harm. They need God's help in their lives as much as you do. Would you not want someone praying for you if you were going down a wrong path? Do you not welcome the prayers of others as you go through this process? Realizing the other person's need for God in their life can help you to begin praying for them. Don't wait until you feel like it, make the choice to do so, just as you had to make the choice to forgive.

**Seventh**—Spend time in God's Word. God's holy Word is meant to teach, inspire, correct, nourish and heal. You can never go wrong by spending time in the Word. Ask God to minister to you through His Word, and in time you will begin to see change.

**Eighth**—Forgive yourself if need be. Sometimes the healing process isn't complete until you can learn to forgive yourself. No one is free from making mistakes. Use those mistakes as learning tools instead of condemning yourself.

**Ninth**—Be patient with yourself. If you choose forgiveness you are on the right track, even if you don't feel it. Over time the hurts will melt away and your healing will become complete. Trust God's process and His timing. Take one day at a time.

Choose forgiveness every time. Forgiveness is liberating! It is freedom! The next chapter may help you make this choice by hearing from other's who also had to choose forgiveness.

To download a free worksheet that goes along with these steps and has room for personal notes, go to:

https://psalm23ministries.com/your-free-gift

# Chapter 10
# You Are Not Alone

My story may not be one you can relate to. This chapter includes stories from others who have gone through trials in their life. Their stories may be different, but the common theme is the rollercoaster of emotions. No matter the story, the end goal is to reach the decision to choose forgiveness.

## Mary's Story

In June 1981 Mary was a young lady excited to plan her wedding which was four months away. But one night she sensed something was wrong. Then her fiancé, Scott, admitted to her that he had been unfaithful the night before. Mary was devastated. She wanted to die. Scott was everything to her. This was too much to handle, so she broke it off with him.

Not long before this, Mary had become a Christian. This newfound faith would be tested but also would be her guiding light. After about a week, Mary reached a decision. She and Scott had been sexually active outside of marriage, so she felt like damaged goods. In her mind she thought her only choices were to become a nun or marry Scott. However, Mary truly felt God had wanted her to marry Scott, so they reunited and married four months later.

Mary enjoyed being a wife and eventually a mother. She would get excited when she heard Scott's truck drive up the driveway after work. But Mary had an insecurity deep within her that never went away. She noticed Scott glance at pretty girls, and she feared that she could be discarded at any moment.

Fifteen years into the marriage Mary was feeling frustrated, exhausted and like a failure. Scott said he thought he knew why and began to confess more of what happened fifteen years earlier. He admitted that he lied about what really happened when he was unfaithful during their engagement. They talked all night, and Scott revealed that he was deep into pornography. She was unfamiliar with the term "sexual addiction" at the time but knows now this is what he was dealing with.

When they finished talking that night, Scott told Mary he had confessed everything, there was nothing more. But Mary felt in her spirit that there was more. The next day he came to her and confessed more, then said that was all. This went on for five days. During this time Mary went about life as if everything was OK, putting on a front to be strong. She even had a family portrait taken with Scott and the kids. She admits this was her attempt to hold something together that was falling apart.

After five days of hearing more and more, Mary told Scott he had to leave. They had a camper in the back of their property, so Scott moved into that. The second night, Scott left a note under the door for Mary. When she read it, she felt like Satan himself had written it. She marched to the camper to confront Scott about the letter. But when she saw him, he had turned into a demon. He kept saying, "I see the blood, I see the blood." The note and this incident scared her so much that she slept with the phone and a gun by her side. She locked all the windows and pushed furniture against the doors. The three older children were staying with a friend when this happened, so only the baby was home with Mary.

Everyone was telling Mary to divorce Scott. But an encounter with God made her believe otherwise. One day the verse "I will never leave you nor forsake you" came to mind. She felt like God lifted her chin, as if to look into her eyes, and emphasized what He had said, "I will never leave *you*, I will never forsake *you*, you need to know that." She hung onto this promise through the difficult times.

Mary decided to get a legal separation, instead of a divorce. She reached out to a friend of theirs who had in the past struggled with pornography and had previously talked with Scott. His words of wisdom struck her. It gave her a fresh sense that God's "got this" and to wait on Him.

After this meeting, she decided to go back to the camper and face Scott again, filled with hope and courage. She didn't know what to expect, but this time she was met with something much different. In front of her was a humble man with soft eyes and a brokenness. He came into the house to talk and poured out his heart. Mary collapsed and spent the next week in bed. She chose to forgive Scott but was unable to unpack all the woundedness it had caused in her. She didn't realize how deep the wounds were, it was just her normal.

They sought counseling, but Mary's insecurity of possibly being discarded at any time or *traded-in* did not go away. She questioned Scott every time she thought his eyes were wandering. Mary says this gaslighted her for the next seventeen years! Scott always said he was fine, there was nothing to worry about and told Mary she was just being insecure and fearful.

The fear of being discarded caused Mary to begin hoarding which was a security blanket to her. She wanted to make sure she and the children would be taken care of and didn't think her husband was going to do that. She describes it like this, "As a squirrel stores nuts for the winter, I stored stuff for the future."

In January 2014 Scott went to Guatemala on a mission trip with the men from their church. While he was gone, it snowed heavily. Mary and her son had to get the tractor out of the barn to plow, but Scott's pickup was in the way. When her son moved the truck, a page of pornography slid out from under the seat. Mary's world fell apart again, and she felt like hell was laughing at her.

The next day she was to fill in for someone in the office at her children's Christian school. She took her Bible and devotional with her to read and the school had Christian music playing. By the end of that day, Mary felt God had truly ministered to her. She felt courageous, at peace and knew God "had her" and it would be OK, even though she had no idea of the future. She chose again to forgive Scott.

While in Guatemala, God also got a hold of Scott. Upon returning home he joined a support group through *Pure Desire Ministries*[1] for sexual addicts. Mary got the workbook for herself but realized she could not do it alone. They offered support groups for women as well, so she joined an online group.

Even though Mary chose to forgive Scott, she describes forgiveness as a choice and a process that needs to be walked out. It did not mean justifying what he had done. Mary admits handling things much better this time. Now she had support from people who understood, instead of blaming her. Previously fear and insecurities caused her to become bitter. Bitterness had stayed with her for about ten of those early years and she struggled with suicidal thoughts. This time she had guided help through the process. Despite all of this, she still was not certain that her marriage could survive, but she was hanging on to hope.

Mary felt deep joy after Scott came back from Guatemala. How could she feel joy? She describes it like this: She had hit rock bottom, was lied to and betrayed. She came to an end of herself and let God be in control. She didn't have the desire to try to be strong anymore. She finally surrendered and believed what God said about her. She played Christian music from sunrise to sunset each day and let it minister to her. This was like putting ear plugs in, so she couldn't hear the enemy lie to her anymore! Mary let God minister to her. She danced to the music and imagined God's arms around her, and they danced. During this time, she felt so much peace and joy, and so deeply loved.

Where are they at today? Their marriage has been restored by the grace of God. Both are still involved with the *Pure Desire Ministries*. In fact, Mary leads multiple groups helping women through this difficult time in their lives. God is opening doors to them to bring good out of this tragic situation. It is also their desire to bring awareness to churches about this taboo subject. They are now empty nesters and Mary is so thankful their marriage has been restored as they enter this new phase of life. Mary stated her heart swells with gratitude for what the Lord has done for her. She doesn't ask God why she had to go through this, she is just grateful.

What a wonderful story of redemption. If Mary was not willing to forgive Scott, on more than one occasion for the same offense, their marriage may have ended. Instead, they are happier then they probably have ever been, and are paying it forward to help others!

## Brian's Story

School was coming to a close and summer vacation was a few days away. A typical school day, with anticipation of summer fun ahead took a tragic turn. As Brian was walking to gym class, an older student came up to him and put his arm around him and said, "Hey let's go talk."

Brian found himself going into the school locker room, then pushed into the shower and molested by this kid. Crying, he ran out and was headed straight to the Dean's office. But in the hallway, he bumped into his brother, who was a year older. He told his brother what happened, expecting him to do something. Instead his brother ran off. So, Brian ran to the Dean's office.

Outside the door the attacker tried to bribe him with a quarter not to say anything, but Brian went in the office and shut the door.

Once Brian told the Dean what happened, his parents were called. They reported it to the police but were told it was probably best not to pursue pressing charges because it would end up in the newspaper. On this advice, his parents did not pursue charges and chose to enroll Brian and his brother in a different school for the next school year.

Doing the right thing by telling what happened, only to be told to drop it, added to the emotional scars. After this happened, Brian learned to suppress his emotions for years, but he didn't trust anyone. Hatred grew in Brian's heart for this guy as the years went by, and for black people in general. The kid that attacked him was African American and Brian says the attack created a lot of racism in him. At one point he wanted to start a clan, and many times wanted to seek this guy out and "take care of him." Thankfully, that never happened.

After fighting with God for years, Brian finally gave his life to Christ. When he did, he said his hatred for the attacker was wiped out. He forgave this man but held on to the shame for many more years. He didn't even tell his wife what happened to him. The scars of what happened affected how Brian parented his children. His wife didn't understand why Brian was so strict about where they were and with whom his children were around. He and his wife were together almost twenty years before Brian told her his story.

At one point, Brian talked with his brother and asked him why he didn't step in and do something on that horrible day. His brother pointed out that the kid who attacked Brian was a gang member. He said if he had tried to do anything, they both could be dead. And at that age, what could he do? This helped Brian to understand his brother's point of view.

About 2012 Brian went on a mission trip with several men from church. The same trip Scott from the previous story was on, only a different year. While on this trip he heard a story about a child raped by her father and impregnated. Hearing this grabbed Brian and opened everything back up. God was tugging on Brian's heart, wanting him to share his story. But every night Brian wrestled with God, not willing to talk. On the last night on the trip, the guys had a time of sharing their "aha moment." Finally, Brian gave in and shared his story. It was hard at first but after he shared, three other men shared they went through a similar situation. He describes it as a God moment.

From that moment on, Brian says the shame lifted from him. Satan kept telling Brian prior to this that he was alone, and he shouldn't talk about what happened. He now sees that you cannot get release until you tell your story; as long as it is kept a secret it has power over you.

Since his trip he has publicly shared his story with his church and talked with his kids about it. Being willing to share what happened has opened so many doors for Brian. His boys understand why he parented as he did, and now they are more open with him. Brian has also had the opportunity to share his story with other men to help them to forgive someone.

No matter where things go from here for Brian, he holds on to the Lord's Word that He will never leave him or forsake him.

What Brian went through is something no child should ever face. The scars that are left behind can stay with a person forever if forgiveness is not chosen. Isn't it ironic that the scripture that

Brian holds on to is the same one Mary does, Hebrews 13:5?

## Julie's Story

This story is different in many ways from the others. One factor is it is a current, ongoing story at the time of publishing this book.

Early on in Julie's marriage she admits she was a Christian but was not living her life for the Lord as she should. Her husband, Neil, did not know the Lord as Julie did, but they did attend church each Sunday. Hanging out with friends, going to the bar and having a few drinks was something Julie and Neil enjoyed doing. Then Julie found out she was pregnant, something she didn't think was possible. She knew from that moment on that she had to stop that way of life and totally surrender to God. She gave up drinking and did not want to go to bars anymore.

Previously, Neil had suffered two strokes which affected his memory, physical strength and the ability to speak in stressful situations. The use of his right arm was limited, and he developed a limp. This also caused him to be unable to determine the difference between social drinking and drunkenness. Though they did not put a zero tolerance on drinking or him going to the bar, Julie did not want to allow intoxication in their marriage anymore. This was not only because of her Christian values, but because they were now parents who needed to set a good example for their child.

Their beautiful, miracle baby girl was born in the summer of 2014. Over the next six months, Neil had come home intoxicated on at least two occasions. She believes he did not intentionally get drunk, but in his mind he was fine. This, in part, stems back to the strokes, as well as the addiction.

That December Neil was not feeling well. The memory loss and fatigue were getting worse. His ability to speak was becoming more difficult. Julie took Neil to the doctor and after examining an MRI, sent him to a specialist immediately. The news was quite shocking. They don't think he had another stroke. Neil was told he only had *one* blood vessel left in his brain, far less than an undamaged brain! The doctors tried to pull vessels from other areas but none of them held. So now Neil would have to manage with one vessel, which was going to require changes in his life. The doctor told Neil if he were to use drugs or alcohol, or even extreme amounts of caffeine (or anything that would over stimulate the brain) that he could have another stroke and end up in a vegetative state. A small amount of caffeine would be OK, but he would have to give up alcohol altogether. Even casual drinking was adding a bullet to the "chamber" which could go off at any time.

Neil was given a regimen to follow along with medications, which did help him feel better. Julie and Neil decided to have a zero tolerance for him going to the bars and drinking. They continued to get together with friends, who would drink around them, but Neil would not consume alcohol. Things were going well for about six months. Then one night, Neil went out with some friends and came home intoxicated. Julie asked Neil to leave. She needed to send the message his behavior was not OK, but she did not want a divorce.

They decided to seek marriage counseling. The counselor was able to help Neil see why going to the bar was not OK, even if he was not drinking. She related it to post traumatic stress syndrome (PTSD) and used a war analogy. The sound of a loud noise could trigger a response in someone to think it was gun fire or a bomb. For Julie, the trigger was the bar. After about three weeks, Neil moved back home.

Another five to six months went by and Neil relapsed and got drunk again. However, this time he did not go home nor did he contact Julie for about three days. He had been staying at his dad's place. After some time to think, he realized he wanted his family back. His dad was an alcoholic who drank until he passed out daily and was all alone. Neil did not want that life, nor did his dad want that for him.

Unfortunately, getting drunk, not coming home for days and emptying the bank account was a cycle that happened about every six months. Each time Julie would forgive him and take him back. She had conflicting feelings, as a wife and a mother, but she loved her husband and wanted her marriage to work. They had bought a home and Julie became pregnant with their second child.

When the baby was about five months old and their oldest child was about 3.5 years, he did it again. This time Neil called from the bar to say he was not coming home. He had also broken his promise to never drink and drive. Julie and a friend, with kids in tow, went looking for him because they did not want him driving drunk and killing someone or himself. While driving around, her daughter sitting in the back, said a prayer. She said, "Dear Jesus, can you give me a new daddy that will love us and won't drink." This broke Julie's heart. She knew her daughter loved her daddy, but she was hurting.

Again, Neil said he wanted his family back. This time they tried a Christian counseling group for alcoholics. He also joined a men's accountability group through his church. Julie was hopeful that having the Christian influence would help Neil. She really believed this time things would work.

They had a weekend planned to go to a 3-day event of stock car racing with friends, something they both enjoyed. This would be their four-year old daughter's first race. Because the events can go late at night, Julie decided not to go Friday night because of her daughter. So, Neil went alone and met up with friends. He and Julie would take their daughter on Saturday.

Midnight Friday night approached, and Julie had not heard from Neil. The races should be finished, and he didn't call or text to say he was going to a friend's house. So, Julie started searching through their phone log to see where she could track him down. What she discovered was unexpected. There were several messages to a phone number she did not recognize. She figured out it was to another woman, someone he had met at the Christian counseling group.

Neil did eventually come home that night, intoxicated again. He confessed that this other woman encouraged him to go drinking while at the race. This was so heartbreaking. Even with all the problems they had faced in their marriage thus far, Julie never expected Neil to have an affair. After this, Julie set limits on Neil's usage of social media. He broke her trust and she could not accept him looking at other women. Yet, she still loved him and forgave him. Neil expressed he wanted his marriage and family to work, but he wanted to be able to continue drinking, and he wanted Julie to go out with him and monitor how much he could drink. Julie could not understand how a can of beer was more important to him than his children, or his life!

Before this last incident happened, they had a weekend trip planned without the kids. Both wanted the marriage to work and were hopeful. Julie recalls telling a friend that *this* time was going to work. She says the affair opened her eyes to how we can take people for granted. It also showed her that even though she forgave Neil, she could have still had an attitude about it. Julie also noted that sometimes we are not conscious of how we talk to someone, so she became more aware of that.

After this trip, on a fall day, Neil was going to run an errand and be right back. But hours went by and he didn't return. At 4:00 AM he showed up at home, very intoxicated. Julie tried to take the keys away from him because she was "done." Neil violently reacted by picking her up by the neck. Their 4-year old saw this and was scared. This was the first and last time Neil assaulted Julie. She grabbed the children, all three in their pajamas, and headed to her parent's house at 5:00 AM.

This was the final straw. Julie made Neil move out, but she still wanted him involved in the children's lives. He had a good spell of seeing the children up to 5 days a week, which eventually faded. Their daughter would call her dad, but often got his voicemail. She has asked her mom "Why can't I have my family back?" How does Julie help her daughter understand, when *she* doesn't fully understand? Neil was to spend Christmas Eve with his children but broke that promise. To date he has not been with his children for about a month.

This story does not have an ending. Julie doesn't know what lies ahead. She can't help but wonder if she will get a call soon that Neil had one drink too many. This is a sad story of addiction destroying a family, repeated forgiveness for repeated heartbreak, and a story of hope. Learning this type of forgiveness is new to Julie and has learned it is a process, one that is ongoing for now. Julie's faith sustains her and trusts that the Lord will see her through.

> **Matthew 18:21-22 (NKJV):** *Then Peter came to Him and said, "Lord, how often shall my brother sin against me, and I forgive him? Up to seven times?" Jesus said to him, "I do not say to you, up to seven times, but up to seventy times seven."*

Here we see Jesus instruct Peter that forgiveness is to be given over and over again. He described it as seventy times seven. The Lord was making a point, that we are to always forgive one another. In Mary and Julie's story, these women had to make that choice to forgive, not once, not twice, but many times.

As you can see, many people are going through something. You may not see it in their lives, but behind closed doors their world could be falling apart. So, you are not alone. Don't keep it bottled up any longer. Let someone know what you are going through. Exposing the enemy's attack against you is the first step to healing, you cannot do it alone! Remember what I said in Chapter 6 about allowing others to help is when you truly are being strong.

In the previous chapter I gave you some tips on how to get started with the forgiveness process. But even when you choose forgiveness, it is still important to work through the emotional side of things. The next chapter will help you with that piece of your healing process.

# Chapter 11
# Self-Check Steps

Have I stirred up a lot of emotion in you? By now, my stories have likely triggered your memories. How are you feeling about forgiveness? That subject alone can stir up a lot of emotion. Tackling the emotional aspect of things is extremely important and will help you with the forgiveness process. What do you want for your future? In this chapter I am going to challenge you with a lot of questions, to help you get to the bottom of your emotions.

Let's look at what your next step should be. I suggest you do what I call a "self-check." Here are 6 steps to follow to examine what you are going through.

**FIRST**—Evaluate how you are feeling right now. What emotions did this book stir up for you? Try to identify each emotion. Are you feeling angry towards someone? Has hurt that you suppressed been starting to resurface? How about revenge? Are you still wanting to get even with someone for what they did to you? Has sadness set in? Are you frustrated about a situation that was never resolved?

**SECOND**—Write down each emotion you are feeling. Take your time as you assess what is going through your mind. Refer to Chapter 2 if you need a little help identifying what that emotion is. Writing each emotion down on a piece of paper will help you to become more aware of it. The act of writing stimulates cells in your brain, bringing the information to the forefront. This can also help with your memory. The more you write the more you recall. This happened for me as I was writing this book. Things I had forgotten came back to me as I started to write my stories.

You may be thinking to yourself that you don't want to remember. I can understand that. But if you refuse to face those things that caused you deep pain, they will always haunt you. You may be able to suppress it and seem to live a successful life, but do you have peace in your life; healthy relationships? Are you held back from pursuing a dream because someone crushed it? If you have not dealt with these issues, allow yourself to remember and push through the pain. There is greatness on the other side of pain.

**THIRD**—After identifying the emotions, look at each one individually. Ask yourself why you are feeling this way. What brought each emotion to the surface? Who hurt you, and how did they hurt you? Be honest with yourself. As I mentioned above, I understand it may not be easy to remember the hurt. Now is the time to face it so you can conquer it. Exposing your pain takes power away from the enemy.

**FOURTH**—Now I want you to ask yourself a very difficult question. Did I play any part in this? Don't get me wrong, when someone intentionally hurts you, they are completely responsible. But sometimes, we may have opened a door.

For example: In my case, I came to realize that I opened a door for Kyle, as well as Jerry, to be abusive towards me. How did I do this? I allowed fear to rule my life, which in turn kept me from taking necessary action. If I would have had the courage to stand up against these two, I would have packed my bags long before they ever had the chance to do anything. But I feared losing my husband; and being on my own. But that's what I got anyway. And by staying in the situation, the fear grew deeper to the point of paralyzing me. Realizing that I had opened doors, made it easier for me to forgive. They made choices that were wrong and very hurtful to me, and they will have to answer to God, as we all will. But I could have prevented it by trusting God instead of letting fear make my decisions for me.

Again, this applies not only to the big hurts, but smaller hurts as well. Can you recall a time when you did not forgive someone? Were you too proud to say, "I'm sorry" to someone? And then your relationship spiraled downhill from there? Have you gone through a divorce? Did you treat your spouse or significant other with respect? Did you degrade him/her in front of others? Were other people a priority over your spouse or significant other? Perhaps you had a falling out with your parents and now have a strained relationship, or worse yet, you haven't talked to them in years.

Looking back at the situation, could it be you blew something out of proportion? Was it really as bad as you made it out to be? Did the person intentionally hurt you? It could be they don't even know they hurt you. Is it possible you are holding onto a grudge for a hurt that only exists in your mind?

Please understand I am not trying to place blame on you for the things you went through or are going through. Nor am I saying what I went through was my fault. These were grown men who made the decision to hurt me. They had two choices, they could choose to hurt me or not, unfortunately they made the wrong choice. What I am saying is I simply made it easier for them to carry out their choice by letting fear make my decisions for me. Understanding this concept can be very freeing.

**FIFTH**—Even if you had nothing to do with the hurt that happened to you, are you prepared to forgive? Are you ready to start the process of forgiveness to whomever, for whatever? Are you ready to forgive yourself, if need be? If not, why? What is holding you back? Could it be fear? Can you honestly say you love your life as it is, and you are content and filled with joy? If you had no negative emotions come up as you read this book, then maybe you have already forgiven that someone and didn't even realize you had. Only you can answer these questions.

**SIXTH**—This step is a hard one as well. I want you to look at this from another angle. Are there possibly hurts in your life right now that may stem from something *you* did to hurt someone? Have you heard the phrase, "You reap what you sow?" There are scriptures that can help explain this.

> **Job 4:8 (NIV):** *Even as I have seen, those who plow iniquity and sow trouble reap the same.*

> **Galatians 6:7 (NKJV):** *Do not be deceived, God is not mocked; for whatever a man sows, that he will also reap.*

Here's a possible example of this: Perhaps you were a bully in school, picking on the weaker kids. Now as an adult, it feels like people are mean to you. Could it be because of your past? Again, this is not aimed at blaming you. The focus is to help you understand the root cause of the pain you are experiencing.

Every decision we make has consequences, some good, some not so good. Reaping what we sow does not always happen immediately. Those consequences could come years later. So, it is not always easy to relate the offense to the consequence.

But there is hope through repentance and forgiveness, and it is called grace. Our Lord is quick to forgive our sins when we repent. Repentance is defined as feeling remorse or regret for something. When the Lord forgives your sins, He does not hold them against you any longer, they are washed away by his blood.

It is important to be honest with yourself. If you have hurt someone, then the first thing you need to do is ask the Lord to forgive you of your sin. There may come a time when you need to talk to that person and apologize. Sometimes that is not possible, as they may have passed away or you no longer know where that person is. Don't worry about that, start with repentance and let God take care of the rest. When we follow God's ways, He is faithful to heal, as the following scripture tells us.

**Psalm 147:3 (NKJV):** *He heals the brokenhearted and binds up their wounds.*

These six steps are a guide to help you reflect and get started on the path to redemption. The process may not be easy, but the rewards will be great! The weight on your shoulders that you have carried over the years will begin to lift. When it does, you will feel such freedom and be ready to receive new beginnings from God! As you read the next chapter of God's restorative power in my life, I want you to start claiming that God will do the same for you.

To download a free worksheet that goes along with these steps and has room for personal notes, go to:

https://psalm23ministries.com/your-free-gift

# Chapter 12
# Restoration

**Psalm 23:3 (NKJV):** *He restores my soul; He leads me in the paths of righteousness for His name's sake.*

Rebuilding my life after not one, but two divorces was difficult to say the least. Fear had become such a normal part of my life that it was hard to trust and believe anything good could happen. Some days the only thing that got me out of bed was the Lord. I hated my life and felt as though I had no purpose and was unlovable.

Rarely a day went by without tears. I was angry with God, especially after my divorce from Jerry. I trusted God to provide for me, believing the judge would make Jerry give me some financial support and pay half of the debt that had accumulated. Instead I was hit with the devastating blow of having to pay all the debt myself without a dime of support from Jerry.

I could not believe God would leave me so destitute. I didn't believe in prayer any more. I was punching the wall in frustration. God had abandoned me, so I thought.

I was forced to work two and three jobs at once, and even a fourth temporary job one year. With that, I still could not make a dent in the debt. Filing bankruptcy was not an option, in my mind. I am not one to shirk my responsibilities, so I was determined to pay off all the debt. That was until I collapsed from sheer exhaustion. This was a turning point for me.

My neighbor's son was graduating from high school that night and I was going to attend the ceremony. When I got home from work, I decided to lay down on the couch to rest. What happened next was unexpected and a bit scary. After laying there for a while I tried to get up and get ready to go to the ceremony. But I couldn't move. My body was going nowhere. It felt as though someone had dropped a truckload of bricks on my body. The exhaustion was like nothing I had ever experienced before, and this scared me. There was no possible way I could attend the graduation. If I had tried, I likely would have ended up in the hospital.

That experience made me reflect upon my situation. Working so many jobs, 2 being full-time was more than my body could handle. Changes needed to be made and made soon. The first choice I made was to break down and talk to an attorney about filing for bankruptcy. That was a hard decision, but I had to accept the truth of my situation. I also had to realize the bankruptcy laws were for people like me in those tough situations and it was OK to use the law for my betterment. I also decided to scale back my business to be on a very part-time basis with only a few key customers.

As I was going through all of this, I felt like such a failure. Things kept compounding themselves. I was faced with another divorce, and I felt shame because of being abused and rape. I felt betrayal, was emotionally spent and exhausted and I was now financially ruined and bankrupt. It was hard to care about anything, I felt worthless. My life was in shambles and I was embarrassed.

The stigma of being abused and raped and not leaving the situation sooner was tough enough. But I carried shame around because of a second divorce. I felt like I was an embarrassment to my family, though they never made me feel that way. Here I was, a firm believer in marriage vows, yet

I was facing another divorce, as if one divorce wasn't bad enough. What were people going to think of me?

I did not think life could ever be good again. I wanted nothing to do with men. Considering the idea of marriage again was completely out of the question for me, nor did I even want to date. I was angry, being left destitute by both of my ex-husbands. I was not going to allow another man to do that to me again.

Thankfully, God was patient with me and continued to minister to me, even while I was mad at Him. I began to catch myself praying to Him one day. This made me realize I do still believe in prayer and in God's faithfulness. I simply did not understand all that happened to me. Even though I felt like God had abandoned me, deep down inside I knew He didn't. If I had a dollar for every time I cried out, "Help me God" I would be rich. I wanted the pain to go away and to feel good again.

As I mentioned in previous chapters, God ministered to me through Joyce Meyer and her ministry. His Word began to touch my heart. God also put wonderful friends in my life to support me and love me. And then that one beautiful day that I was able to say, "I'm happy" blossomed forth from God's grace. Jesus was restoring my soul, as the scripture says at the beginning of this chapter.

A better word than saying I was happy is to say I had joy. Happiness is an emotion, felt for a short time due to a circumstance. Joy, on the other hand, is deep down within your spirit brought on by a relationship with Jesus. It can sustain you through a tough time, if you allow it. Consider the following scripture:

> **Nehemiah 8:10 (NKJV):** *Do not sorrow, for the joy of the Lord is your strength.*

Restoration is a slow process as well. Think about restoring an old house where things are falling apart, paint peeling, failing appliances, and so much more. To bring that house up to a restored status, one must plan, study, research, work patiently and diligently. Rushing the job could potentially create more problems and the end result won't be the desired result. When following the right process, and the house is complete, it is so beautiful. People will be in awe of the transformation. It will look and feel like a new home.

That analogy is what I went through. As much as I wanted to rush the process and get rid of my pain, that's not how it happened. God had to give me bits and pieces or it may have been too overwhelming to absorb. He knew what to give me and when to give it to me. There were days I wanted to run away and hide out on a secluded island or a remote cabin because I hated my life. It seems God always showed Himself to me in a special way on those most difficult days.

Something worth mentioning is that even though Jesus ministered to me, my healing required my participation. The Lord is not a genie in a bottle that you call upon to grant your wish. He won't wave a magic wand and make all your troubles go away. He wants a relationship with you, and anyone who has been in a relationship knows that it requires participation.

I had to spend time in prayer, listen to worship music and praise my Almighty Father. I had to spend time in His Word, attend church, allow others into my life and trust the Lord and His process. I had to choose to forgive and I had to do a lot of repenting. You see, some days were better than others. Some days I didn't want to do any of these things. I'll be honest, there was a war going on inside. At times I had good days, feeling a ray of hope. Then there were the times where I would get depressed, hopeless, and angry at those who hurt me and questioned God. I wish I could say the healing process, once it started, went smoothly. The reality of it is the process was a roller coaster. I had a lot of deep wounds and the Lord had to work through each of them. This process took years.

If you are coming out of a broken relationship, I strongly urge you to avoid entering a new relationship right away. The wounds associated with that broken relationship must be dealt with for complete healing. If they are not, then it is much harder, if not impossible, to have a healthy relationship with another person. The baggage from the first relationship gets carried into the next. Typically, it will surface at some point in the new relationship. It may take years and you may not even realize that the root cause is unresolved feelings from the first relationship. Don't be too eager to move on with someone else. Take the necessary time for yourself to heal. You are worth it! However, I also caution you to not use that as an excuse for years, to not move on with your life. You will need to find a healthy balance of giving yourself enough time to heal and when to start letting others into your life.

And don't try to do this without Jesus. Invite Him into every area of your life.

My attitude towards men began to change as the Lord helped me heal. After about two years I realized I did want to date again, and I even wanted to marry someday. I enjoyed the institution of marriage, as God designed it. But I was in no hurry for that, and I wasn't about to go looking for a guy. I prayed about it and told God I wanted Him to choose someone for me when I was ready and when the guy was ready for a relationship. Friends wanted me to join an on-line dating site, but I wanted nothing to do with that. For me, I felt like that would be *shopping* for a guy instead of trusting God to choose someone for me. I'm not saying God can't use a dating site to connect two people, I'm just saying it was not a tool that I felt comfortable with. I wanted the good old-fashioned way of meeting.

For eight years I went about rebuilding my life and my relationship with Jesus. Then one day I received a message from Pastor Greg's wife. There was a guy that attended their church in Illinois that she and Pastor thought I should meet. They felt the two of us might be a good fit and she wanted me to visit them so I could meet him. I told her I was not interested, that a relationship would just complicate my life. I left it with God and said to Him, "If you want me to meet this guy then you will find a way to bring him to me." At the time I was starting a new job, sold my house and was looking to buy a different home closer to work. I ended up renting a house and when she found out about it, I was contacted again. In the meantime, Pastor was working on Duane with his "sales" pitch. They had attended a baseball game together and he told Duane about me. I finally agreed to let Duane contact me through social media.

A couple of weeks after that he traveled from Illinois to meet me and attend a wedding with me. Wow! God did hear my prayer and answered it! The relationship started off very slow. I was very cautious, plus he had his own past of hurtful relationships, so trusting did not come easy for either of us. After two years of long-distance dating, he proposed, and I moved to Illinois and we married.

Two lives brought together by the restorative power of our Lord Jesus Christ. I continue to thank the Lord for bringing Duane into my life. His desire is to serve the Lord and be the best husband he can be to me. Duane is very involved with the church, in various capacities and I am proud to be married to a man with a servant's heart.

My brothers seem to think Duane spoils me! I guess that is a huge compliment to Duane. Not sure I'm willing to admit I'm spoiled, but he certainly treats me with the utmost respect, chivalry, and deep love. He is my best friend who makes me laugh and I love being with him. Jesus is the center of our marriage and He has given us both new beginnings and restored our lives. Duane has his own restorative story to tell, but that is for him to tell. What God has done in our lives is nothing short of miraculous.

Glory to God, this is only the beginning of my story. Most of my life I have been very shy and insecure. I've been purposeful to work on these areas of my life for many years and see Jesus continually transforming me. I have had the privilege of being in a position of leadership in my church, helping in the community and developing many new relationships. Writing this book is one more way that the Lord has stretched me and given me a new opportunity to trust Him. After both traumatic times in my life, I said early on I hoped that some good would come from what I went through. That prayer is being answered in a big way. There has always been some good, the transformation in me alone has been good. But I wanted to help others too. Before this book was even completed, I had the opportunity to help people with their hurts.

I am so excited for the new doors He is opening to me. What lies ahead is unknown, but I know it will be exciting and good! I could do none of this in my own strength. But through Him I can do whatever he calls me to do.

> **Philippians 4:13 (NKJV):** *I can do all things through Christ who strengthens me.*

I hope this brings a ray of hope into your heart. God has a divine plan for your life, and it is meant for good!

## Chapter 13
# God's Plan for You

**Jeremiah 29:11-12 (NKJV):** *For I know the thoughts that I think toward you, says the Lord, thoughts of peace and not of evil, to give you a future and a hope. Then you will call upon Me and go pray to Me, and I will listen to you.*

This scripture should bring joy to you, knowing your heavenly Father has thoughts of peace towards you. His thoughts include hope and a future for you. That future can be bright if you allow God to work in you and through you by trusting and being obedient to Him.

This has always been one of my favorite scriptures. For most of my life I didn't know what type of career I should pursue. I have never had that overwhelming passion to have a certain career or ministry that many people experience. This has been discouraging at times. But this scripture has always reminded me that even if I couldn't "see" what I was supposed to do, God still had a plan for me. He will reveal to me what I need to know, when I need to know it. I won't lie, sometimes it has been hard waiting on God to show me what I should do next.

How about you? Do you have a dream or a vision to do something that seems out of reach? Do you feel underqualified to do it? I hope that whatever hurt you have gone through has not derailed that dream of yours. If it has, it may be time to start thinking about it again. Or maybe you are like me and still don't know what you want to do with your life or are supposed to do. Have you asked God about it? It may be time to talk with God. Pray about it and wait on Him.

Surrendering *your* plans and asking God what His plans are for you can be scary. But His plans are always bigger and better than what we could think. Surrendering is an act of obedience. Obedience to God can open doors to receive the blessings of God.

It could be your dream has not come true yet, because God is waiting on you. He is waiting for you to ask Him into your plans. However, if you continue to harbor negative thoughts towards someone, you may not be able to hear from God about your future.

Committing to forgiveness and repentance releases the power of Jesus Christ to come into your life and transform you. Hold on to your hats when you do that, because the Lord has an amazing ride for you. But don't be impatient. God may promise you something, but He probably will not promise *when* you will see it. Do you know the story of Abraham and Sarah? The Lord spoke to Abraham when he was 75 years old telling him he would have a son, but that son did not come for another 25 years. Abraham was 100 years old when his son was born! That is a long time to wait for God's promise, but God was faithful. And Abraham never lost hope in God. He knew that if God said He would do something, then it would happen.

It is time to shift your focus. No more dwelling on the past or the hurts. Instead, it is time to believe that God your Father loves you immensely and has a wonderful plan for your life. Grab hold of it! When the devil whispers in your ear, don't listen! Speak out affirmations such as, "I am a child of God. He loves me unconditionally. I am forgiven, the past is behind me. He has a plan for my life and that is for good, not evil." Remember the spoken word has much power. Here is a scripture verse you may want to recite:

> **Psalm 139:14 (NKJV):** *I will praise you, for I am fearfully and wonderfully made; marvelous are your works, and that my soul knows very well.*

Here is another story that shows how God can take something terrible and use it for His glory, bringing about blessing. After reading this story, think how your heavenly Father can take your bad situation and use it for good. This is a snapshot of the story, you can read Genesis chapters 37–48 for the complete story.

Joseph was only 17 years old when his life-altering event happened. He was the youngest son of Jacob, and the favorite of all Jacob's sons. Joseph's brothers were jealous of him because they could see their father loved him more. They schemed to kill him, but instead put him in a pit, then sold him off.

From there, Joseph was taken to Egypt to be a slave. He was then bought by Potiphar, the King's officer. He saw that Joseph had favor with the Lord, so he made him overseer of his home. But the pit Joseph had been in before, was not the last of his troubles. He ended up in prison for being falsely accused of seducing Potiphar's wife.

While in prison he continued to have the Lord's favor, being given authority over all the other prisoners. He interpreted dreams of the king's chief butler and chief baker (who had also been thrown in prison). After their release, Pharaoh had a dream and they told him about Joseph interpreting their dreams. This prompted Pharaoh to send for Joseph to interpret his dream. The interpretation was that there was to be seven years of good crops, followed by seven years of famine.

Pharaoh then made Joseph overseer of his house, and all the people to be ruled according to Joseph. Only Pharaoh's throne would be greater. Joseph was given authority over all the land of Egypt (and he was a Hebrew slave)!

When the famine came, Joseph's brothers came for help. Because of what his brothers had done to him, Joseph could have turned them away. Instead he loved on them and saw to it that they were well taken care of. He had forgiven them.

Wow! What a story. Joseph would have every right to be a bitter person for all the wrong that was done to him. But instead of harboring bitterness in his heart, he was forgiving. And look how God blessed him. It is a wonderful story that I suggest you read. Think of what God can do in your life!

Are you ready to let go of the past, and let God fulfill your future? God has given you talents and gifts, how can you use them? The dreams you have will likely use those gifts. Let God lead you into the future that He has set before you. Your dream may be tweaked a bit by God, or he may have something much bigger for you than you can ever imagine. Whatever it may be, if you seek God first, He will be faithful to show you what to do and bless you in many ways.

> **Matthew 6:33 (NKJV):** *But seek first the kingdom of God and His righteousness, and all these things shall be added to you.*

The Lord may also be asking you to serve others to help develop within you, obedience to Him. I believe serving is a way of seeking God's kingdom. No matter what you are going through, keep God front and center in your life daily. God knows your needs as well as the desires of your heart. Often when you are willing to let go of trying to control a situation (and this can include control through worrying), that is when God will allow that blessing to flow to you. He is waiting for you to trust Him and commune with Him.

> **Matthew 20:26-28 (NKJV):** *But whoever desires to become great among you, let him be your servant. And whoever desires to be first among you, let him be your slave, just as the Son of Man did not come to be served, but to serve.*

> **Jeremiah 29:13-14 (NIV):** *"You will seek me and find me when you search for me with all your heart. I will be found by you," declares the Lord.*

Before you know it, doors will start to open for you. New beginnings, new relationships, and a deeper love for your savior Jesus Christ. Be prepared for that "exceedingly, abundantly above what you could ask or think" to start coming to life.

**Malachi 3:10 (NKJV):** *Bring all the tithes into the storehouse, that there may be food in My house, and try Me now in this, says the lord of hosts, if I will not open for you the windows of heaven and pour out for you such blessing that there will not be room enough to receive it.*

Look at me, never in a million years did I ever dream I would be writing this book. But one day the Lord strongly laid it on my heart to write this book to help others be released from captivity. I had no idea how to write a book, I was clueless. But God is faithful and brought the right people into my life to teach me. And he spoke to me throughout this process. I couldn't have done it without Him.

He also used my amazing husband to encourage me. In fact, my husband had more faith in me than I did. I was quite nervous and felt under-qualified to write a book. But both he and God knew I could do it, if I let God lead me.

Our Father in heaven is waiting to bless you. Are you ready to receive? Are you ready to let God heal your broken spirit so you can experience God's boundless joy? Think about that, boundless, unlimited, immeasurable joy! Do you want that in your life? Invite the Lord into your situation. And don't be afraid to dream big. Remember, it could be that the Lord is waiting for you to ask Him for help. So, ask Him to teach you, to give you a sign, give you the courage, or whatever else it is you need from Him. Ask Him what His plan for your life is (not yours). Look at this scripture:

> **Isaiah 55:8-9 (NKJV):** *"For My thoughts are not your thoughts, nor are your ways My ways," says the Lord. "For as the heavens are higher than the earth so are My ways higher than your ways, and My thoughts than your thoughts."*

God has a plan for your life that is exceedingly, abundantly more than you can think of. I am so excited for you to be released from the grip of unforgiveness and start a new life in the Lord.

My walk with the Lord has only grown deeper through the trials and tribulations I have gone through. Writing this book is one way to bring something good out of something bad. As the scripture says:

**Genesis 50:20 (NKJV):** *But as for you, you meant evil against me; but God meant it for good, in order to bring it about as it is this day, to save many people alive.*

God will take your bad situation and turn it around and allow good to come from it, if you let Him, as He has for me.

Blessings to you in your next chapter of life. Don't lose faith, be patient and don't forget to include God. He is standing by, waiting for you to invite Him into your life, into your situation. You are never alone!

I would like to close with a prayer for you.

*Heavenly Father, I lift up each person reading this book. They may be dealing with a painful situation in their life right now, or they may know of a loved one that is in pain. Send your Holy Spirit to minister to them right now. I pray they will feel your presence and your peace wash over them. Minister to them in their time of need. Let hope start to fill their hearts again. May your Word bless them and speak to them. Help them through the process of forgiveness and learning to move past their emotions. I pray they begin to see how precious they are to you and that you do have a plan for their future, a plan that is meant for good. Restore their souls unto you. I ask this in your name, Jesus Christ. Amen.*

# Conclusion

There was a lot of material in this book meant to guide you on a path of healing. You are deeply loved by Jesus Christ who came to this earth as a vulnerable child to experience the things we experience. He was ridiculed, mocked, rejected, mobbed, wrongly convicted and eventually tortured for your sins and mine, though he was free from sin.

Jesus was sentenced to death, and willingly accepted that sentence so that you and I would not have to pay the ultimate price for our sins. As it is written in scripture:

> **Hebrews 12:2 (NKJV):** *Looking unto Jesus, the author and finisher of our faith, who for the joy that was set before Him endured the cross, despising the shame, and is set down at the right hand of the throne of God.*

His joy came from knowing that He could spend eternity with us if He would endure the cross. It was a brutal death He suffered for all mankind. What an amazing, selfless act of love Jesus displayed for us.

Don't let the past rule your life any longer. Make the commitment today to go through the process of forgiveness and take back your life. Let today be the first day of new beginnings and a deeper walk with the Lord Jesus Christ. There is greatness within you, not your greatness, but the greatness God put in you for His purpose. He's just waiting on you to reveal it.

Please share this book with anyone you know that needs help moving past their hurts and the emotional pain they hold on to. Anyone struggling with unforgiveness in their heart needs to be set free!

The book is available at Amazon.com for purchase in a variety of forms. I would also like to ask that you please leave an honest review of the book on Amazon.com. Your feedback is appreciated.

Thank you so much for wanting to make positive changes in your life! May God's blessings be upon you.

# Notes

*Chapter 2. Gamut of Emotions*

1. Cockrell, Thad & Brandon Heath (2012). Hands of the Healer [Recorded by Brandon Heath]. On *Blue Mountain* [CD]. Brentwood, Tennessee .

*Chapter 6. Who Can I Trust?*

1. *Enjoying Everyday Life* television series, by Joyce Meyer, www.joycemeyer.org.

2. *Battlefield of the Mind, Winning the Battle in Your Mind*, author Joyce Meyer, FaithWords Edition, Copyright 1995 by Joyce Meyer Life In The Word, Inc.

3. *Living Beyond Your Feelings*, author Joyce Meyer, FaithWords Edition, Copyright 2011 by Joyce Meyer.

## Chapter 7. God Winks

1. *Hallmark Movies & Mysteries*, owned by Crown Media Holdings (2015).

2. *A Godwink Christmas*, written by John Tinker and David Golden, released in 2018, inspired by the series of books by Squire d. Rushnell, and inspired by the series of books by Louise DuArt.

3. Squire D. Rushnell, author and inspirational speaker.

## Chapter 8. Forgiveness Is Not!

1. Webster's New World Dictionary of the American Language, College Edition, (Cleveland and New York: The World Publishing Company, 1966), s.v. "forgiveness."

2. Webster's New World Dictionary of the American Language, College Edition, (Cleveland and New York: The World Publishing Company, 1966), s.v. "forgive."

3. Reagan, Will (2009). Break Every Chain [Recorded by Will Reagan and the United Pursuit Band]. On *In The Night Season* [CD]. Knoxville, Tennessee.

## Chapter 10. You Are Not alone

1. *About Us.* (n.d.). *Pure Desire Ministries.* retrieved December 17, 2018 from https://puredesire.org/pages/who-we-are

# Bibliography

*About Us*. (n.d.). *Pure Desire Ministries*. retrieved December 17, 2018 from https://puredesire.org/pages/who-we-are

Cockrell, Thad & Brandon Heath (2012). Hands of the Healer [Recorded by Brandon Heath]. On *Blue Mountain* [CD]. Brentwood, Tennessee.

Gifford, K. L., Angel, D., Shepard, M., & Arnot, K. (Executive Producers), Robinson, M. (Director). (2018). *A Godwink Christmas* [Motion Picture]. United State: Marvista Entertainment.

Hallmark Movies & Mysteries. Crown Media Holdings (Owner). October 2015. United States: Los, Angeles, California.

Joyce Meyer Ministries. *Enjoying Everyday Life* [Television Series]. Daystar Television Network.

Meyer, J. (1995). *Battlefield of the Mind, Winning the Battle in Your Mind*. New York, NY: FaithWords Edition.

Meyer, J. (2011). *Living Beyond Your Feelings*. New York, NY: FaithWords Edition.

Reagan, Will (2009). Break Every Chain [Recorded by Will Reagan and the United Pursuit Band]. On *In The Night Season* [CD]. Knoxville, Tennessee.

Rushnell, Squire D. author and inspirational speaker.

*Webster's New World Dictionary of the American Language, College Edition*. Cleveland and New York: The World Publishing Company, 1966.

# About the Author

Kathy Bates has a passion to help others better their lives, so they can experience the life God has for them. She is involved with her local church as a leader with the First Impressions Ministry, a barista at the church's coffee shop, manages the content of the church website and phone app, has been involved with the choir and Christmas musical. She also loves to get involved with special events at her church.

Kathy was also a volunteer and later employee at the local pregnancy center, ministering to women who found themselves in a tough situation. She believes every life is valuable, as well as the unborn.

Jesus is her Savior, inspiration, strength and constant guide throughout her life. Becoming an author would not have been possible without the Lord's direction. She is thankful for the gifts God has given her.

The Lord inspired Kathy to start Psalm 23 Ministries to further minister to people suffering from hurts in their lives.

She resides with her husband, Duane in Illinois. They love to be outdoors, enjoy traveling, and exploring new places. Kathy also loves to scrapbook, sew and do crafts.

\* \* \*

## Contact Information

For speaking engagements, questions or comments, the author may be contacted at:

Email: Kathy@psalm23ministries.com

To follow Kathy Bates and her ministry please check out her social media platforms.

Facebook:
http://bit.ly/Psalm23Ministries

Instagram:
https://www.instagram.com/psalm23ministries/

# Receive Two FREE Worksheets!

## 6 Self-Check Steps and
## Steps to Forgiveness

This is my gift to you to say thank you
for purchasing this book.

These worksheets correspond with
chapters in the book.

They are tools to help you start
your healing journey.

Receive your free gifts today by going
to the link below:

**https://psalm23ministries.com/your-free-gift**

SELF-PUBLISHING
SCHOOL

## NOW IT'S YOUR TURN

**Discover the EXACT 3-step blueprint you need to become a bestselling author in 3 months.**

Self-Publishing School helped me, and now I want them to help you with this FREE WEBINAR!

Even if you're busy, bad at writing, or don't know where to start, you CAN write a bestseller and build your best life.

With tools and experience across a variety niches and professions, Self-Publishing School is the <u>only</u> resource you need to take your book to the finish line!

### DON'T WAIT

Watch this FREE WEBINAR now, and
Say "YES" to becoming a bestseller:

**https://bit.ly/BestSellerFreeWebinar**

41164869R00124

Made in the USA
Lexington, KY
05 June 2019